Is That You, Grandpa?

Legacy of a British Colonial Dalliance

CHRISTOPHER L. MARTIN

Fulton Books, Inc.
Meadville, PA

Published by Fulton Books 2021

ISBN 978-1-64952-935-0 (paperback)
ISBN 978-1-63710-224-4 (hardcover)
ISBN 978-1-64952-936-7 (digital)

Printed in the United States of America

'Tis looking back that gives the future colour,
Because, in life, we find
The past analogizes all the future
Upon the plastic mind;
Foreshadowing what "will be," and what "had been,"
A mingled repetition
Of words and deeds, events, and many a scene,
And fantasy and vision

Egbert "Leo" Martin, 1860–1890, my father's relative

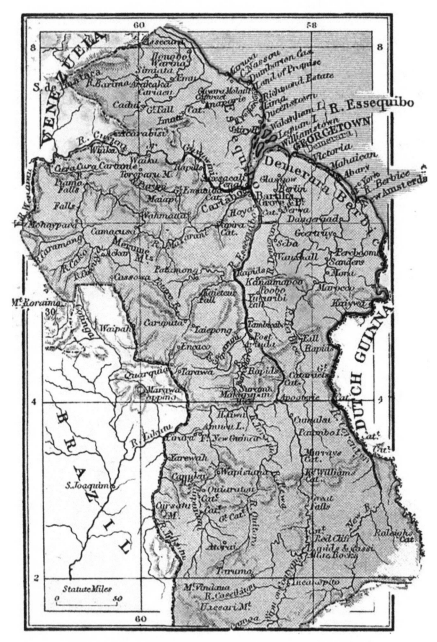

Asprey's Atlas of the World (London: Asprey and Co., Ltd., 1920). Courtesy the private collection of Roy Winkleman.

Contents

PREFACE

My mother, Ruby Edith Camilla Pollard, a mulatto, was born in Georgetown, British Guiana,[1] reputed to be the storied "El Dorado" where, according to the famed explorer Sir Walter Raleigh, the streets were paved with gold.

Ruby's mother, Julia Amelia Pollard, was the daughter of a freed African slave, Hilda Chapman, and Josiah Pollard, manager of a sugar or rice plantation in British Guiana.

Ruby never knew her father. She was Julia's illegitimate daughter with, according to family lore, "a German Jewish diamond merchant employed by a British diamond syndicate." Ruby recalls her mother revealing that her father's name sounded like "Speight." Herr Speight had come to British Guiana in 1897–1898 looking for diamonds and, in addition, found Julia, with whom he fell in love. Julia soon became pregnant by him. He told her that, if she bore him a son, he would give the child his name, pay to raise him, and educate him in England. A daughter would not bear his name nor receive the same educational benefits. Although Speight said he would provide for a daughter financially, Julia told him emphatically that he could keep his money. During her pregnancy, and after my mother's birth, Grandpa's agents tried to deliver packages to her, but she refused them. Julia was but the first in a continuing line of strong, independent women in our family.

Ruby, born on May 19, 1899, was not the son Herr Speight longed for. He soon left British Guiana and returned to Europe where,

---

[1] British Guiana was renamed Guyana in 1966 when it achieved independence from Britain.

again according to family lore, he died not long after of Blackwater Fever, a complication of malaria acquired in British Guiana.

Around 1935, Ruby married Alexander Adolphus Donovan Martin. Together they had three children: Claire (now deceased), Christopher (me), and Anthony. Before she died in Albany, New York, where she spent her last years with Claire, Mommy told Claire that, when she was about twenty years old, she had a dream about her father. Never having known him, she described to her mother what he looked like in her dream—short and bald—and her mother confirmed her description. Mom never dreamt of him again.

Ruby was very precious to us, and before she died in 1989 at the age of ninety, we promised each other that we would find out who her father was.

This book is a search to find Ruby's father, our grandfather.

A.A.D. "Bertie" Martin (fig. 1)

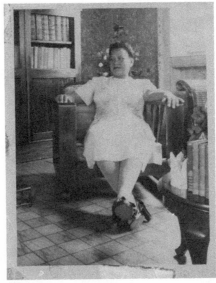

Ruby Martin in a Berbice Chair ca. 1949 (fig. 2)

CHAPTER 1

Our Family Tree: The Donovan/Martin Clan

A multitude of national, religious, and ethnic entities

My sister, Claire Patricia Theresa Martin-Combs, was born on August 10, 1936. As you would expect, given that my father was a man who loved women, Claire was his heart.

I made my debut the following year, at home in Georgetown, British Guiana, on September 13, 1937, the first son and second child of Alexander Adolphus Donovan (Bertie) Martin and Ruby Camilla Pollard Martin (fig. 1 and 2). Upon hearing this happy news from the attending midwife, my father, usually a commanding and dictatorial person, exclaimed, "I have a son," and promptly passed out.

Tony, or Anthony Adolphus Donovan Martin, the last of Bertie and Ruby's children, was born on May 24, 1939.

Our family tree has a multitude of ethnic, religious, and national roots: African Zulu, African "Winkel," Irish Catholic, East Indian Hindu, German Jewish, Dutch Protestant, Sephardic Jews (from Portugal and Spain), and Ashkenazi Jews (from Eastern Europe).

My paternal heritage

My paternal grandfather, Alexander Adolphus Martin, was born in 1867. He earned his livelihood in many ways, first as a clerk in the Guianese gold fields, then as a salesman at the Singer

Sewing Machine Company, and finally as a machine pattern maker at Sproston's Foundry and the Diamond Sugar Plantation. Over 150 friends and family mourned Conrad—as he was affectionately called—at the funeral service at his residence, 224 New Market Street, Georgetown, on June 29, 1941.

Before marrying my grandmother, Constance Donovan, Conrad fathered a daughter, Mabel (May) Barnwell, of whom he was very proud (fig. 3). Before he married Constance, he required that she accept May as part of the "package," and agree that May would continue to enjoy all the rights and privileges of being Conrad's daughter.

Grandpa Alexander Martin and daughter Mabel
(May) Barnwell ca. 1900 (fig. 3)

At the time they were married, Constance was a much-respected nurse in Georgetown and a pillar of the Catholic Church.

Together, Conrad and Constance fathered a son, Bertie (my father), and a daughter, Iris (fig. 4).

Alexander and Constance Martin with Bertie and Iris ca. 1914 (fig. 4)

Constance Donovan had her own multiethnic heritage. She was one of four daughters of Hester (Ma) Donovan, a white Creole Barbadian of Irish Catholic descent whose wealthy family had at some point immigrated to Barbados. There is no documented evidence regarding Hester's ancestry, but one of her descendants believes she was the granddaughter or great-granddaughter of Sir George Pyle (or Pile) of Great Britain and Barbados.

Why Hester came to British Guiana in the late eighteen hundreds is a mystery. According to family lore, she was disinherited and banished by her parents in Barbados after becoming pregnant by one of the Negro carriage horse-grooms. We do not know if Donovan was Hester's family name or whether it was the name of a man who fathered one of her children. Regardless, it seems reasonable to assume that "Donovan" was her maiden name and that she gave that surname to all four of her daughters: Constance, Clarice, Elizabeth, and Olive.

Ma Donovan was stern looking and somewhat severe. In a photograph taken in her later years, her hair is pulled back tightly from her face and forehead and tied in a bun in the back of the head (fig. 5). She was a tall, statuesque, broad-shouldered, authoritative figure.

Ma Hester Donovan (fig. 5)

Ma's granddaughter, Audrey Holder, recalls that Ma was not very endearing. While Ma was living with Audrey's family, she and Audrey's father, John Brevel Holder, got into a dispute because Ma was rough on Audrey, his only daughter. He rebuked his mother-in-law and reportedly cut off communications with her for a long time. Consequently, Ma Donovan left the Holder household and went to live with Constance where she remained until she died in September 1934 at close to one hundred.

Another granddaughter, Violet, reported that Ma was somewhat of a tyrant. She demanded that Violet say "Yes, Ma" to her call. A mere "yes" was met with a retort to say, "Yes, Ma" or else "you would get a licking."

As Ma became older, she spent a lot of time alone in her room. When friends came to visit, she would often quip, "Well, [so and so], you came to see this old lady? Come in." And they would go to her bedroom to chat.

Constance was Ma's first child and probably was conceived in Barbados. Her Irish heritage dictated that she become a committed Catholic, and in her later, less ambulatory, years the Roman Catholic Bishop often visited to celebrate Sunday Mass at her home altar.

Constance and Conrad's daughter, my aunt Iris, followed the same rigid Catholic religious practices: Mass at Church every morning, confession every Friday, Mass and Communion on Sunday. Aunt Iris was so steeped in the practices of Catholicism that she remained single, and presumably chaste, until she was in her early fifties, at which point she married a Seventh Day Adventist Minister in his mid- to late seventies. He passed away a few years later. Thankfully, Iris's mother Constance did not live to witness the apostate religious conversion of her daughter (fig. 6).

Aunt Iris and Claire (fig. 6)

Conrad's first daughter, my aunt May, had two sons, Ulric and Carl. Grandfather Conrad adored them, and they lived their formative years with him and Constance, even when May emigrated to the United States.

My father, Alexander Adolphus Donovan Martin, was born in November 1905 and died in 1958. Everyone who knew him called him Bertie. He was a civil servant but also a serious student of English language, literature, Greek, and Latin.

He pursued his avocation as a dramatist by studying for a year at the Bristol Old Vic Theatre School in England in the early 1950s, became the director of the Georgetown Dramatic Club, and cofounded the Georgetown Theatre Guild—the first such organization in British Guiana. Daddy's relative, the celebrated Guianese poet, Egbert ("Leo") Martin, was a great inspiration to him. He loved the language of Egbert's poems, which is quintessentially Victorian English, clear evidence of the British culture that surrounded and nurtured him.[2]

My maternal heritage

Before Mummy died, Claire recorded several interviews with her about her life. According to Mummy, her grandmother, Hilda Chapman (my great-grandmother and Julia's mother), was pure African, purportedly a Zulu. She was born on the Hague Estate, one of many Guianese plantations. Her husband was a mulatto, born in Georgetown of Dutch/English heritage. Her uncle, Phil Pollard, was a prominent businessman in Georgetown in the 1890s, either a plantation owner or manager.

Julia was born around 1862 and died in 1934 at the age of seventy-two. At some point after my mother was born and my grandfather left British Guiana, Julia married John (or Samuel) Applewhite (or Applewaite). He was a native of Barbados and, according to Ruby, a very good stepfather to her.

---

[2] There are three known books of Egbert Martin's poems: *Leo's Poetic Works*, 1883; *Scriptology*, 1885; and *Leo's Local Lyrics*, 1886.

CHAPTER 2

Tony's Research

Looking for Grandpa

My brother Tony began "looking" for Grandpa in October 2007 via Google. His search words (alone or in combination) were typically "Speight," "Diamond Syndicate," "British Guiana," "Blackwater Fever," and similar terms.

We learned from newspaper reports and history books that in the last few years of the 1800s there was a "diamond rush" in British Guiana. We also discovered that a diamond syndicate, Wernher, Beit & Co., acquired leases of substantial acreage as part of an effort to acquire and control the Guianese diamond fields and diamond production.

We knew that Grandpa was a "German Jewish diamond merchant," indicating that he might well have enjoyed a position of authority within the syndicate. He never married Julia, and we have no written record of his surname, but we knew from what Julia told Ruby that it sounded like "Speight."

In Tony's search, the name "Speight" never surfaced, but the name "Alfred Beit" appeared repeatedly. The phonetic similarity of the two names, Speight and Beit, captured Tony's attention.

Although he avoided publicity and is not a "household name" by any means, Alfred Beit was a heavyweight in the South African diamond and gold mining industries. He was a very close associate of

Cecil Rhodes, after whom Rhodesia was named,[3] incorporated, with Rhodes, DeBeers Consolidated Mines Ltd., and eventually became one of the wealthiest men in Europe.

We also found the timing of Alfred Beit's death intriguing. We know that Mummy's father left British Guiana in or about 1900, shortly after Mummy was born, and he died just a few years later. Alfred Beit died prematurely in 1906 at fifty-three years of age.

These facts were a start, but they were just the beginning of our search to unravel the mystery of our grandfather. Tony kept searching and eventually compiled the timeline of Alfred Beit's life that appears in Appendix 1. His timeline, however, left us with the question, "Where was Alfred Beit in mid-1898 when Mummy was conceived?"

---

[3] Rhodesia is an historical region in Southern Africa whose formal boundaries evolved between the 1890s and 1980. White settlers first used the name "Rhodesia" to refer to the region in the 1890s, informally naming their new home after Cecil Rhodes, the founding and managing director of the British South Africa Company (BSAC) which governed Rhodesia until the 1920s. Newspapers used the name from 1891, and it was made official by the company in 1895 (*Wikipedia, Rhodesia,* accessed 11/3/20).

CHAPTER 3

De Beers in British Guiana. Why?

Sir Walter Raleigh's "El Dorado"

The 1890s spawned a confluence of events that directly affected my ancestors. To understand this narrative of a family in a remote part of the world, British Guiana, one must come to grips with the intersection of African slavery, British colonialism, Indian, Portuguese, and Chinese indentured servitude, the influence of Dutch culture and engineering ingenuity, German and Jewish involvement in the precious metal trade, and the dominance of an Irish expatriate woman, my paternal grandmother, and a German Jewish diamond merchant, my maternal grandfather.

The legacy of slavery in British Guiana

The name "Guyana," originally British Guiana, derives from an Amerindian word meaning "land of many waters."

In his sixteenth century writings, Sir Walter Raleigh called the country El Dorado ("the Golden"), and its streets were said to be paved with gold. It was at various times occupied by the Dutch, the French, and finally the British.

In 1752, the Dutch, the first settlers to arrive in Guiana, established Fort Zeelandia as the capital of the Essequibo and Demerara Regions (fig. 7).

Ruins of Fort Zeelandia (fig. 7)

The fort was an edifice complete with cannons overlooking the Essequibo River to protect the area from foreign invaders sailing up the waterway. Figure 8 shows a sign at Fort Island with a picture of the Fort. Figure 9 depicts the Court of Public Policy, which also doubled as a church, and a farm that still exists is shown in figure 10.

Sign at Fort Zeelandia (fig. 8)

Policy Hall at Fort Zeelandia (fig. 9)

Farm at Fort Zeelandia (fig. 10)

Subsequently, Guiana was divided into three separate countries, British Guiana (now Guyana), Dutch Guiana (now Suriname), and French Guiana (now Cayenne). French Guiana is the site of the infamous prison on Devil's Island where Captain Alfred Dreyfus was incarcerated. The prison was also featured in the 1973 movie *Papillon*.

The lush climate of all three of these countries lent itself to the development of vast sugar, rice, fruit, and vegetable plantations which not only fed the growing demand for these crops and their by-products (rum, for one), but required huge numbers of laborers. Thus, British Guiana, like most of the North and South American countries and the islands of the Caribbean, fed and benefitted from the ever-growing African slave trade.

The British outlawed slavery in 1834, destroying the country's source of cheap labor to work its lucrative sugar and rice plantations. This resulted in the importation of a failed succession of indentured servants from China and Portugal.

Former African slave societies developed in different ways in British Guiana after emancipation in 1834. Some freedmen went into the civil service and were trained by a succession of British colonials under a British governor. They pursued their education at prestigious secondary schools, Queens College and St. Stanislaus College in Georgetown, the capital. They adopted the Christian religions of the Portuguese and British.

Some slaves moved into the interior where the indigenous Amerindians lived off the land. They were called "bush negroes." There were other slaves who had been carpenters, bricklayers, coopers, and artisans, and who hired out their services. They were known as "Winkel" slaves, and many had actually gained their freedom before emancipation. They lived in New Amsterdam, a major city. There is still an area in New Amsterdam called Winkel. Given my grandfather Conrad Martin's childhood in New Amsterdam and his technical skills and professions, it is reasonable to assume that he must have come from "Winkel" ancestry.

Finally, the British government tapped another of its colonies and brought thousands of impoverished laborers from India. These immigrants proved more successful at harvesting the crops, and by the end of the nineteenth century, British Guiana had become one of the most ethnically diverse countries in the world.

Intermarriage and other liaisons created a people of mixed heritage and multiple religions. Hindus and Muslims from India tended to live in the rural areas where the great rice and sugar plantations were located, and they lived mostly in harmony, maintaining their ties to the land and their religions, building mosques and temples.

Secondary education in the rural villages was scarce and, with notable exceptions, their lives centered on an agrarian economy. It was a hard existence, not very different from that of the earlier African slaves. That they came to prosper as shopkeepers, doctors, lawyers, and other professionals against daunting odds and oppression was a testament to their indomitable will.

When I was about fifteen or sixteen, around 1952, Daddy found me a job working as a weigher in a sugar-cane plantation. When the cane plants were ready to be harvested, the fields were set on fire. This burned off the leaves and cooked the cane stalks, making them soft and juicy for compression in the liquidation process.

My job was to sit by the "punts" (flat bottom boats) and record the tare weight of each laborer before he started work. Then he would enter the field, cut the cane, and return, filthy with soot, with piles of cane on his head for weighing at my station on the riverbank. Once I calculated his loaded weight, he would dump the cane into a punt and return for another load, and another, and another, repeating this backbreaking labor until the whistle sounded for lunch or at day's end. These laborers were either Pakistani or Indian and were often referred to by the derogatory name "coolies."

One day one of the laborers, with whom I had become friendly, invited me to lunch at his home located on the banks of a small stream. His home was a typical structure—twelve by twelve feet, with mud and straw walls and roof, a single slatted wood window and a door (fig. 11). There were no interior partitions. A woodstove stood in the center of the room, and there were neatly stored hammocks hanging on the walls. The smell of curry goat cooking on the stove was divine.

Painting by E.R. Burroughs (renowned Guianese artist) of typical East Indian sugar cane workers' huts (fig. 11)

The worker introduced me to his infant children and his gracious wife, who was slapping roti between her hands to make it flaky. It was obvious to me that they had spent a considerable portion of his meager wages on this meal, and except to ask him if he had any other children, I said nothing because I was ravenously enjoying the authentic Indian curry.

My silence gave him the opportunity to talk about his five other children. To this day, I am astonished by their accomplishments. He had five grown children who either had finished university or were completing their degrees. The oldest was a barrister who studied law in England. He returned to practice in Georgetown and to help two remaining siblings in university abroad, who were studying engineering and medicine. Another son was a dentist in the US who was also contributing to the education of other siblings still in school.

The shibboleth that the poor have little ambition or drive was again refuted many years later and a continent away when my employer, Allied Chemical Corporation, asked me to recruit for senior MBAs at Atlanta University, an HBCU (historically black college and university).

During my interview with a young graduate, she revealed that she was the last of her fourteen siblings to earn her college degree. I was amazed and felt the financial burden on her parents would be too onerous unless they were very well-off financially.

I asked her, "So, what do your parents do for a living?"

She replied in a mellifluous Southern drawl, "They're share-croppers, Suh."

So much for those who impugn nonwhites as not being ambitious and hardworking. These two emblematic experiences have shaped much of my admiration and hope for the hardworking poor.

Gold and diamonds in British Guiana

In 1890, one Edward Gilkes, while prospecting for gold along the Putareng River in the upper course of the Mazaruni River in British Guiana, found a few diamonds in the batea (a pan) he used for gold washings (Swiecki 1).

Between 1890 and 1900, between two thousand and three thousand diamonds were found, but no large stones or extensive numbers of diamonds were found. In his travel account *The West Indies and the Empire; Study and Travel in the Winter of 1900–1901*, H. de Rosenbach Walker wrote:

> The West Indian Colonies continue, as in the past, to be devoted almost entirely to agriculture. The principal exception is British Guiana on the mainland, where hopeful anticipations are held as to the future of the gold industry…I heard a good deal also about diamonds, and since I left, there are said to have been sensational discoveries.

However that may be, the Jews were arriving and the De Beers Company were going to get a report from some of their experts. (Walker 53–55)

De Beers was, of course, the company that Beit and Rhodes had incorporated (more on this in ch. 5, infra).

Several newspaper articles confirm the intervention of overseas involvement in the diamond discoveries in British Guiana, and even in the United States in the late 1890s and early 1900s. Here are some examples:

> "13,000,000 for a Mine—Camp Bird, Col., Property Bought by English and American Syndicate" The *New York Times*, September 18, 1900

> DENVER, Sept. 17. It was announced to-day that Thomas F. Walsh will receive $13,000,000 for his Camp Bird Mine at Ouray, Col., from a syndicate of English and American investors, headed by Alfred Beit, the South African diamond king, and J. Pierpont Morgan...John Hayes Hammond, the mining engineer, arrived at Ouray to-day to make a final examination of the mine on behalf of the syndicate.

"Diamonds in British Guiana"
The *New York Times*, January 12, 1901

> The mail from Demerara [British Guiana's main county where the capital Georgetown is located] brings a report of large finds of diamonds in the interior of British Guiana. A company has been formed in England to work the claims.

Systematic digging for diamonds began in 1900 when the British Guiana Diamond Syndicate obtained a concession of 2000 acres and started operations on a tributary of the Mazaruni River. Later the Mazaruni Company was granted 5,858 acres in the same area. During a period of six weeks in 1901, a New York company found 8,227 small diamonds. By 1903, there were 27 companies working in the Mazaruni River fields. (Walker 53, Swiecki 2)

My own research at the Bureau of Lands and Mines in Guyana in 2007 revealed that Guianese diamond production went from zero in 1900 to 8,500 metric carats in 1901 to a high of 220,260 metric carats in 1923. One of the recurring themes in all the historical documents I read was that, once diamonds were discovered, De Beers had to control by good means or bad every diamond operation in the world, including Russia, to keep its stock of billions of dollars in diamonds viable. Diamonds have no intrinsic value. Their value is set by control of supply vs. demand. In his research, Tony found a lot of information on what has become known as "the diamond invention." As Edward Epstein explains in the preface to his excellent book, *The Diamond Invention*:

The invention is far more than merely a monopoly for fixing diamond prices; it is a mechanism for converting tiny crystals of carbon into universally recognized tokens of power and romance. For it to ultimately succeed, it must endow these stones with the sort of sentiment that would inhibit the public from ever reselling them onto the market. The illusion thus had to be inculcated into the mass mind that diamonds were forever—"forever" in the sense that they could never be resold.

The invention itself was a relatively recent development in the history of the diamond trade. Up until the late nineteenth century, diamonds were a genuinely rare stone. They were found only in a few river beds in India and the jungles of Brazil. The entire world production of gem diamonds amounted to only a few pounds a year.

In 1870, however, there was a radical change in this situation. Huge diamond "pipes" were discovered near the Orange River in South Africa.

These were the first diamond mines ever discovered. Now, rather than finding by chance an occasional diamond in a river, diamonds could now be scooped out of these mines by huge steam shovels. Suddenly, the market was deluged with a growing flood of diamonds. The British financiers who had organized the South African mines quickly came to realize that their investment was endangered: diamonds had little intrinsic value, and their price depended almost entirely on their scarcity. They feared that when new mines developed in South Africa, diamonds would become at best only a semi-precious gem.

As it turned out, financial acumen proved the mother of invention. The major investors in the diamond mines realized that they had no alternative but to merge their interests into a single entity that would be powerful enough to control the mines' production and, in every other way that was necessary, perpetuate the scarcity and illusion of diamonds. The instrument that they created for this purpose was called De Beers Consolidated Mines, Ltd., a company incorporated in South Africa.

As De Beers penetrated and took control of all aspects of the world diamond trade, it also assumed many protean forms. In London, it operated under the innocuous name of the Diamond Trading Company. In Israel, it was known under the all-embracing mantle of "the syndicate." In Antwerp, it was just called the CSO—initials referring to the Central Selling Organization (which was an arm of the Diamond Trading Company). And in Black Africa, it disguised its South African origins under subsidiaries with such names as the Diamond Development Corporation or Mining Services, Inc. At its height, it not only either directly owned or controlled all the diamond mines in southern Africa, it also owned diamond trading companies in England, Portugal, Israel, Belgium, Holland and Switzerland. (Epstein, *Invention*, Prologue)

At Christmastime, 2007, my wife, Anita, and I went to Guyana with my sister Claire and her husband, Sam. As well as touring Guyana (fig. 12), we visited the public library, a disappointing experience, and the Bureau of Lands and Mines, a more educative visit. There, thanks to the help of Cathy Hughes, later a prominent member of the Guyana parliament, and our guardian angel on the trip, we met with Beatrice Alison Roberts-Austin, a thoroughly delightful and helpful librarian. Her ancestor, "Quelch," was an influential explorer and writer in British Guiana during the 1890s and would have been in contact with the diamond explorers of that time. When I am next in Guyana, I will be doing some research on his writings.

Claire at Kaiteur Falls, 2007 (fig. 12)

We diligently searched the bureau's records, looking unsuccessfully for information on Alfred Beit's possible activities in Guiana during 1898. Although my search at the time was not fruitful, I did stumble upon a note from the mid-twentieth century that referred to a local miner's complaint against the De Beers Diamond Syndicate's monopolistic practices against competitors through strict control of supply, demand, and pricing. At the time, I had not heard about the "diamond invention" and wondered how the company was able to do that until I later came across a March 1, 1903, article from the *New York Times.* It is a fascinating and cogent account of the worldwide diamond industry at that time, indicating that De Beers was mining and controlling all but 3 percent of the entire diamond output of the world as a result of Rhodes's, Barney Barnato's (another diamond investor) and Beit's consolidation of more than three thousand private South African claims into De Beers Consolidated Mines Ltd. (*The New York Times*, March 1, 1903). This was further evidence to me that it was likely that Beit, as a principal in De Beers, was part of the diamond exploration activities in British Guiana in the late 1800s.

We were also encouraged to find De Beers was in fact present during the early stages of diamond discovery in the 1890s and the start of production there in 1901. Later, I found additional evidence that Wernher, Beit & Co., another company formed by Alfred Beit (with his good friend, Julius Wernher), was exploring for diamonds in British Guiana in those years. A written reference in the British Colonial Records Book, British Guiana (vol. 5, 1902) reads:

> We must not forget that Wernher, Beit & Co., after prospecting in British Guiana (see minutes on 7089) abandoned the enterprise as not likely to prove sufficiently remunerative. (Colonial Record Book, 1902)

It was time for us to expand our search.

CHAPTER 4

My Search In London

Oxford's Bodleian Library, the Cotswolds, and the Mitford Sisters

Tony's findings led me to visit the New York City library, Howard University's Moorland–Spingarn Research Center, New York's Schoenberg Library, the Library of Congress, and finally the United Kingdom, Oxford University and other British archives. The purpose of this hunt was to answer the question: "Where was Alfred Beit in 1898, between July and September?" Answer this question and, just perhaps, we will have found Ruby Pollard Martin's father, our grandfather. Thus, in late March 2010, we travelled to the United Kingdom and the vaunted halls of Oxford University.

After a seven-hour trip on a 9:00 p.m. Sunday night flight from Newark on Virgin Air's huge airbus, we landed at Heathrow Airport near London after ten on Monday morning. With two suitcases, a computer, two overnight bags, and Anita's usual complement of several months of newspapers, we lugged our way to the nearest "tube," where we boarded the Piccadilly Line to Cockfosters.

We disembarked at the Gloucester Road Station, dragging our luggage in multiple trips up what seemed like endless stairs. We finally reached street level and the Millennium Gloucester Hotel, which was, thankfully, just across the street. After checking in around noon, we both collapsed in bed.

Around four in the afternoon, Anita awakened me, and after many protestations, refusals, swearing, and her threat to go out to dinner without me, she got my attention, and I hurriedly showered and dressed.

Next, we took the District Line to the Embankment Station for a cruise down the River Thames to the Tower of London. On the way, we passed the Parliament Buildings and Big Ben, the St. Paul's Cathedral, designed by Sir Christopher Wren, and the London and Tower Bridges. Boating past the recently constructed replica of Shakespeare's Globe Theatre, I was reminded that Daddy had signed the original building's register in 1951 or 1952 when he was a drama student at the Bristol Old Vic. We continued past the London Eye Ferris Wheel, the UK's most popular attraction. Visited by over 3.5 million people a year, it is a breathtaking feat of design and engineering. Passengers in the London Eye's capsules can see up to 40 kilometers in all directions. Then it was back to the hotel to prepare for dinner at a restaurant recommended by the concierge.

As we walked along streets lined with posh townhouses toward Brompton Court, Anita realized that Richmond College was in the neighborhood. Her daughter, Kirsten, spent her junior year studying there. After a twenty-minute walk, we finally reached the Falconiere Italian Restaurant on Brompton Court. The bill was about 52 pounds and well worth it. The meal was a ten and belied the richly deserved reputation for atrocious cuisine for which the Brits are famous. Food in England after that meal was thoroughly anticlimactic.

The next day we started our epic quest for "Beit in '98" at the British Museum of Newspapers in the Colindale section of North London. After an adequate American buffet breakfast, we took the Circle Line to Embankment, changed to the Northern Line to Edgware, and got off at Colindale Station. The museum was half a block on the right from the railroad station on the left hand side of the street. After two trips in the tube and poring over an array of maps, we became accomplished tube rats. Equipped with my new-found commuter prowess, I was emboldened to direct a mystified tourist when to exit the tube.

Thanks to Tony's research and his suggestion that we focus our search of the British Guiana newspapers on the year 1898, we arrived at the Newspapers Museum around noon on Tuesday March

30, 2010. We were greeted by a pleasant Trinidadian gentleman who checked our bags, pens, and coats and engaged in friendly West Indian reminiscences with me. After putting in my request for the *Demerara Daily Chronicle* microfilm for August through September 1898, I began my research. It was a laborious exercise, and I was time-limited, since we had tickets to see *Oliver* on Drury Lane back in the London theatre district that night.

In the British Guiana newspapers from the late 1800s, there were almost daily recordings of gold finds, with individual finders' names and ounces recorded. The records for the period are meticulous. For example, the number of deaths and their causes were often published. Sunday May 1, 1898, reported "constitution disease, cancer, phthisis, anemia, tuberculosis, and rheumatic fever" as the most frequent, in that order. Other snippets included the following: Wednesday May 4, 1898, "Capture of an American liner by Spain. WAR," "Entertainment at the Assembly Rooms," "Mr. Rhodes on an Anglo-American Alliance, strongly favors"; Friday May 6, 1898, "The Demerara Dramatic Club. Patronage of His Excellency Sir Walter J. Sendall, at the Assembly Rooms," "The gold Industry. Accounts entered at the Office of the Department of Mines…Syndicate…143 ounces"; Tuesday, May 10, 1898, "The following passengers booked to sail by RMS *Elk* for Southampton…"

Because of my time constraints and the hour and a half it took staff to deliver the above microfilm, I was unable to check The *Argosy*, 1880–1907, the *Mining Gazette* (1893–1897), or the *Demerara Daily Chronicle Mail Edition* (1898–1916). We left dissatisfied, knowing that we had barely scratched the surface and had not advanced very far in our reading.

Wednesday turned out to be an overcast, intermittently rainy day. Anita and I decided to take a train to Oxford rather than rent a car—a wise decision. After our buffet breakfast, we were on our way. It was a short two-stop ride on the tube to Victoria Station and an hour's train ride to Oxford.

England is a relatively small country by American standards, but the countryside between London and Oxford is quite beautiful and extensive, with a plethora of farms. Londoners sent their children away to such safe havens during World War II when the Nazis were bombing their city. As we passed over the beautiful countryside, I couldn't help but harken back to my youth, and remember that, were it not for the indomitable Brits and their Prime Minister Winston Churchill during the early stages of the war, we would all be speaking German.

I snapped out of my reverie as we reached our destination. We then checked in at Rhodes House at the Bodleian Library at Oxford University, and after some initial confusion, the woman in charge found the documentation that Lucy McCann, archivist at the library, had left for us.

Months before I had e-mailed McCann and obtained the necessary forms, completion of which would allow us to look at original documents at Rhodes House. Once we arrived at the Rhodes House and passed through security, a fascinating world opened up to us.

On the front of the building, there are two plaques denoting the sponsors of the building. One plaque recognizes Cecil Rhodes, and the other recognizes Nelson Mandela. As we entered the foyer, we proceeded through a rotunda with the names of fallen World War II heroes who were Rhodes scholars. Straight ahead was a huge hall dedicated to Rhodes and Mandela. A plaque at the entry identifies the original trustees of Rhodes House, including Alfred Beit and his brother, Sir Otto Beit.

Inside the hall are large paintings of Nelson Mandela on one end and Rhodes on the other. Along the sidewalls are a few pictures of prominent Rhodes scholars, including President Nelson Mandela and President Bill Clinton. After snapping a few pictures, Anita and I proceeded to the second floor to begin our research.

Thanks to Anita's expertise as a former reference librarian, we were able to get access to the Book of Contents prepared by the Royal Commission on Historical Manuscripts. This became our roadmap to identifying the location of specific letters between Beit and Rhodes. Once I started going through the various "folios," I came upon original letters from Alfred Beit to Cecil Rhodes from the late nineteenth century. It was a unique moment in my life. Sitting in the quiet reading room on the second floor of the Rhodes-Mandela

House at Oxford University, I realized I was looking at original letters from a man who might have been my grandfather.

For example, there was a July 1898 letter from Beit to "Rhodes" (as he addressed him) from a location other than on the De Beers letterhead address, which he has crossed out and over which he had written another location that I couldn't make out, explaining why "Phillips and Leonard cannot authorize the publication of Merriman's letter, with reference to the elections and to financial matters." I was mesmerized, more by the fact that these were the actual handwritten letters, than by the contents of the letters (Appendix 2).

In his book *Alfred Beit: A Study of the Man and His Work—1932*, G. Seymour Fort presents the most complete picture of Beit I have been able to find. Fort goes to great length to illustrate the self-effacing, secretive nature of Beit's personality and life, and the paucity of information about his movements and actions. Unlike Rhodes, who strode about building an empire, Beit operated in the shadows, providing the money to build the railroads in Rhodesia and to create the De Beers diamond monopoly and other financial institutions that rivalled and surpassed all in Europe.

Reading Beit's letters, I was beginning to get a sense of him, as though he was in the room with me. Oh, if only he could speak to me. If only he could answer me one way or the other—are you, or are you not my grandfather? The three of us need to know, for our mother's sake. Your kind and generous nature has been well documented, as has our mother's. But your whereabouts between July and September of 1898 continue to elude us.

After several hours plowing through the Bodleian documents, we returned to London, filled with suspense as to what tomorrow's research would disclose.

Thursday dawned with a sight we hadn't seen since we arrived in the UK: SUN, or as Anita asked, "What is that big, bright-orange ball in the sky?" This time, we decided to brave the British highways and drive to Oxford. We went to pick up our rented car, one with the steering wheel on the right. When I observed to the cabbie that I would have to get used to driving on the wrong side of the road, he delivered with aplomb the usual British response: "It's you Yanks who drive on the wrong side."

We all had a good laugh, and we felt like long lost buddies. He told us how cheaply he and his wife could buy quality products in the US. In fact, they visit Las Vegas every year to buy our stuff and pay for their trip with the savings. It's much cheaper for them even when they add in the airfare. Imagine that.

After we checked into the car agency and received dire warnings not to risk a heavy fine by straying into the central city zone, we proceeded hesitantly to try to find the motorway to Oxford. Although we made a few wrong turns, we avoided the "forbidden zone," and luck finally put us on the motorway. I began to display a certain arrogance about my skill in driving on the "wrong" side and negotiating the roundabouts, every American's worst driving nightmare.

We were late arriving at Oxford and found Lucy McCann expecting us. She was most delightful, courteous, and helpful. As fellow librarians, she and Anita hit it off very well. I continued the research I had started the day before. I made copies of the relevant pages in the "Report on Correspondence of Cecil John Rhodes (1853–1902)," which synopsizes the various letters from Beit to Rhodes. Lucy's assistant, a very pleasant and pretty young woman, arranged for me to get Beit's actual, original letters reproduced and mailed to me in the US. I couldn't wait to see and decipher Beit's almost illegible handwriting. I subsequently did receive the letters and learned from some later correspondence with other Beit descendants who live in the UK that they were unaware of the existence of these documents, which I have since shared with them.

We did not find a "smoking gun" during that visit. However, our search proceeded, our faith endured, and we continued to hope that Alfred Beit's voice would speak to us, by and by, from the grave. Until then, it was on to Stratford-upon-Avon to see Shakespeare's *King Lear* at the Courtyard Theatre.

I was impressed that many of the cast members were Black. The cast included Greg Hicks as Lear, Kathryn Hunter as the Fool, Kelly Hunter as Goneril, Lear's daughter, Clarence Smith (a Black man) as the Duke of Cornwall, Ansu Kabia (another Black man) as the Duke of Burgundy, and Tunji Kasim (also Black) as Edmund. The theater was reminiscent of the one in the 1998 movie *Shakespeare in Love*. It is what Daddy used to call "theatre in the round," and it must have been here that he learned some of his craft while a student at the Bristol Old Vic.

The show was over around ten forty-five, and we were off in the middle of the night to find our hotel in Stow-on-the-Wold in the Cotswolds. Despite the fact that we had a GPS system, we became hopelessly lost and kept coming back to Stratford. We called the hotel and advised them that we would be very late checking in. Finally, Providence, not the GPS system, got us there at one thirty in the morning, cold, hungry, tired, and still adjusting to the time change.

The next day, April 2, would be the start of a new and exciting adventure during our quest for Alfred Beit. We would meet with Professor David Dabydeen at Warwick University to discuss one of the nineteenth century's most illustrious Victorian poets, my distant relative, Egbert ("Leo") Martin. David and his colleagues, Ian McDonald and Dr. Letizia Gramaglia, were writing a complete work about Leo and I had played a small role in their research.

Egbert Martin, a Creole, was born in Georgetown in 1861, the son of Richard Martin, a journeyman tailor. He was confined to an invalid's bed for most of his short life and died at the age of twenty-nine in 1890. Nonetheless, writing from his confinement under the pen name of "Leo," he became an extraordinarily well-known poet. Much admired by Lord Tennyson, he gained a degree of international prominence in 1887 when he won an empire-wide competition for adding two verses to the British national anthem to celebrate Queen Victoria's Golden Jubilee. The great Puerto Rican/American historian collector and bibliophile, Arthur Schomburg, described him as "one of the greatest Negro poets in history" (Dabydeen, *Wikipedia*).

David Dabydeen and his colleagues are enamored with Egbert's work and wish to restore him to his rightful place in the pantheon of Victorian poets. A new complete edition of Leo's writings with a scholarly foreword about his life and art is urgently needed to preserve and acknowledge his great contribution to Victorian literature.

We spent a memorable afternoon with David, his family, and his colleagues hearing all about my wonderfully talented relative and their efforts. It doesn't get any better than this.

Saturday we moseyed around Bourton-on-the-Water, where, for five quid apiece, I bought two old issues of *The Cricketer* from 1950 and 1952 at a flea market, with news and scores from some of the great West Indian cricket matches of the day. In the 1951–52 season, British Guiana vs. Barbados, British Guiana won by an inning and ten runs. In the first inning, Ken Walcott was caught by Comacho and bowled by Patois for 59 runs. N. E. Marshall was stumped by Jordan and bowled by Chase for 134. Barbados had 397 in the first inning and 285 in the second. Gaskin had a combined 60 overs and nine wickets with 18 maidens. In their first and only inning, British Guiana had a total of 692 runs for nine wickets declared, thanks to a record setting first wicket stand of 390 runs by L. Wight (262 not out) and G. Gibbs (216, caught Taylor, bowled Greenidge). Greenidge had four wickets in 47 overs and four maidens. Talk about memories.

I remember the great matches for "The Ashes" (the World Cup of Cricket) between England and the West Indies, with Len Hutton for England and the three Ws—Weeks, Walcott, and the man dubbed the "Poet of Cricket," Sir Frank Worrell of the West Indies. I often think about the fact that I have not seen a single cricket match since I left British Guiana in 1957 to come to Howard University in the US. I've got to correct that.

We left Bourton-on-the-Water, where the shallow River Windrush flows through the village under a series of beautiful low arched bridges. I thought about my friend, Tommy Alexander, a Morristown, New Jersey, native and our plans to develop an historic village walk and boating facility along the Pocahontas River, one of the most scenic, beautiful, and hidden sights in Morristown.

I momentarily snapped out of my reverie as Anita and I retrieved our car from the paid parking lot. We then drove to Lower Slaughter for a traditional English tea.

Lower Slaughter is a quaint little Cotswolds town, with narrow roads, stately churches, and the Lower Slaughter Manor. Our five o'clock tea consisted of English scones and clotted cream, an assortment of small sandwiches (cucumber, egg salad, ham, and smoked salmon), and a variety of teas. The maître d' was a very proper gentleman whose elegant and precisely tailored suit seemed out of place on an Englishman. Their preferences seem to run more toward more loose-fitting Harris Tweeds from the Outer Hebrides. My suspicions were confirmed when I detected a French accent.

Anita was in her element; she loves the grace and formality of the English tea, and I must admit I enjoyed the cucumber sandwiches, the tea with cream, which must have been recently milked, boiled, and skimmed, and the tiny sugar substitute balls no bigger than the head of a pin. While having tea, I thought about my dear friend, Adrienne Bliss Brown Greenberg, and how she would have loved this. After about an hour, we returned to Fosse Manor and finished packing for our return trip to Newark the next day, where my eldest son, Deryck, would meet us at the airport.

Back in the US—the Mitford Connection

As it turned out, Adrienne Brown and I did later share tea. She took me into New York for a memorable event at the English Speaking Union. There, I would meet Lady Deborah Mitford, the Duchess of Devonshire, one of the infamous Mitford sisters. Another of these sisters was reputed to have been a friend of Hitler during World War II. Even here, Alfred Beit's presence was felt. The Duchess was a first cousin of Lady Clementine Beit, wife of Sir Alfred Beit, "our" Alfred Beit's nephew.

Most mornings on my way to breakfast at the Morristown Deli, I would walk past the Swiss Chalet, that sinfully delicious palace of the best éclairs I've ever tasted since my mother's. The cream inside is atypically real, and the pastry is exactly crisp. I try to avoid the temptation of going in, except when my friend, Adrienne, is sitting in the window reading her vast array of newspapers or holding forth for those of us who can't resist hearing the latest gossip about local politicians. We share our tidbits with her, and she processes it all and shares the complete version with us. Her high school days at the very exclusive Gill School, and her debutante years as the daughter of wealthy parents, have made Adrienne an authority on the history of the glory days of Morristown and its New York millionaires during the gilded years of the nineteenth century. Numerous trips to England and France and other places in Europe, and her friendship with the gentry there, have made her an intriguing source of stories about the personalities and mores of British society, and we have had many exhilarating conversations on the subject. I shared some of my Alfred Beit research with Adrienne, and she filled me in on the Beit connection to the famous Mitford family.

Deborah Mitford was the youngest of six daughters and one brother. In 1941, she married Andrew Cavendish, the second son of the Duke of Devonshire. Andrew inherited the Dukedom and its vast estates after his older brother, Billy Cavendish, was killed during World War II, making Deborah Mitford, unexpectedly, the Duchess of Devonshire. Billy Cavendish had been married to Kathleen Kennedy (Kick), President John Kennedy's sister. Deborah Mitford's father had a brother, Clem, whose daughter's name was Clementine. Clementine married Sir Alfred Beit, nephew of "our" Alfred Beit.

Alfred Beit never married and had no legitimate children. Upon his death in 1906, he left much of his considerable fortune of over eight million pounds and his invaluable collection of European impressionist art to his mother, his younger brother, Otto, and his sisters. Upon Otto Beit's death in 1930, he in turn bequeathed much of the Beit collection to his son, Sir Alfred Beit, 2nd Baronet.

Sir Alfred subsequently moved to Ireland, and his home there, Russborough House, was a popular tourist attraction, partially because it housed the Beit art collection. Also because of the art collection, Russborough became a target of the IRA.

An IRA gang led by Rose Dugdale, a former debutante from a prominent family, was the first to burglarize it. Among the nineteen stolen art treasures were a Goya, a Vermeer and a Gainsborough. The total haul was worth an estimated 8 million Irish pounds. The gang pistol-whipped both Sir Alfred and Lady Clementine and threw them down a flight of stone stairs. The police eventually recovered all the paintings (Albrecht 100).

Then, in 1986, a Dublin criminal, aka "The General," robbed the house again. He stole eighteen paintings valued at 18 million Irish pounds. The police recovered all but two in Britain, Belgium, and Turkey.

In 1987, Sir Alfred and Lady Clementine donated most of the art collection to the National Gallery in Dublin. Nonetheless, in 2001 and in 2002, there were additional burglaries—seven more paintings were stolen, including a Gainsborough and two Reubens. At that point, more of the collection was moved to Dublin, thus reducing the appeal of Russborough House as both a tourist attraction and an IRA target (100).

Sir Alfred Beit died in Dublin in 1994 at age ninety-one, and Lady Clementine Beit died ten years later. A devoted couple, they had no children (*New York Times*, May 16, 1994).

Like her older, more controversial sisters, the Duchess Deborah Mitford Cavendish became a prolific author. Shortly after the 2010 publication of her last book, *Wait for Me*, the Duchess's book tour was the occasion for a tea, discussion, and book signing at the English Speaking Union. Not surprisingly, Adrienne is a member of the ESU, and she arranged for me to accompany her to the event. I was happy to go, even though I was not particularly eager to hear English aristocracy reminisce about Britain's colonial superiority, and concluded that I would be bored by some starchy British aristocrat. Was I in for a rude awakening!

Our trip into New York took about forty minutes and was filled with the lively chatter Adrienne and I usually engaged in. The ESU was relocated about five years ago to an imposing New York brownstone on E. Fifty-Ninth. Since Anita and I drive often to New York to the Metropolitan Opera and the New York Philharmonic, navigating New York's traffic was not an overwhelming challenge. Upon entering the ESU, Adrienne and I took our seats in the second row of an intimate auditorium about ten feet from the Duchess and her attractive young niece, Lady Charlotte Mosley.

After a brief introduction by Ms. Lopez, the ninety-year-old Duchess launched into a mesmerizing discussion of *Wait for Me*. She talked about her five older sisters and their nickname for her, "Nine."

Even in adulthood, they still called her by this teasing appellation to indicate that she had never progressed intellectually beyond the age of nine. It was obvious that she dearly loved her siblings, even with all their eccentricities and at times alarming behavior, which, in some cases, bordered on treason. She spoke about her sisters with a unique degree of humor, a twinkle in her eye, and a mischievous smile, revealing the beautiful nine-year-old she had been. Now, at ninety, the Duchess was still beautiful, regal, charming, intelligent, and worldly.

One funny story concerned her sister Decca, who had married under circumstances difficult for her parents to stomach. Decca had moved to California with her new husband and was a committed communist. After a thirteen-year separation from Decca, the Duchess went to California for a visit. She found her sister "trousered" and speaking with an American accent. The Duchess described her stay with wry humor, especially the thoroughly uncomfortable dinners: "Tuesday with communists, Wednesday with communists…" It was a bravura performance, and I could not wait to have the Duchess autograph a copy of her book. Thanks to Adrienne's intercession, I was also able to discuss briefly with Lady Charlotte Mosely, the Duchess's niece, my Egbert Martin poetry project. She showed great interest but, unfortunately, was unable to help me with it.

At that point, we still had no proof of Alfred Beit's exact whereabouts in late 1898, I still had a lot to do to help with David Dabydeen's opus on Leo, and I was determined to continue my quest as long as it was feasible. After all, I was having the time of my life.

CHAPTER 5

Alfred Beit: The Early Years

Kimberley Mines: 1853–1888

To appreciate fully the extraordinary trajectory of Alfred Beit's life, his incredible journey from middle class to multimillionaire, and his tremendous contribution to the development of South Africa, it is important to understand the effect that the discovery of diamonds had on what was then an underdeveloped country.

The Development of South Africa

Before the British landed and colonized the Cape Colony in South Africa in 1806, it was a Dutch colony, poorly run and teetering on the edge of bankruptcy (Meredith 1).

Britain's initial interest in the Cape was its strategic location as a naval port to protect its interests in Southern Africa against its French enemies. At that time, the descendants of Dutch, German, and French Protestant Huguenots were the major foreign inhabitants of Southern Africa, the French Protestants having escaped Catholic persecution after revocation of *The Edict of Nantes* in 1685 (3).

These early settlers numbered only about 25,000 and were scattered over an area of 100,000 square miles. Slaves from the indigenous Black African population, and slaves from other African and Asian territories and countries, provided the labor to make the areas prosperous. Cape Town's population at the time consisted of 16,000 people, of whom 10,000 were slaves (1). The settlers spoke Afrikaans, a modified form of Dutch, and were called Afrikaners or Boers (an Afrikaans word meaning "farmer").

Among the laboring population serving the early white settlers from Europe were the indigenous Khoikhoi, or Khoi aboriginal people of South Africa. They were descendants of the original people of South Africa, hunter-gatherers who had become "pastoralists." They were called "Hottentots," and in appearance and color, they were Black Africans, with some Asian features (fig. 13).

Khoikhoi Girl (fig. 13)

In the South African Boer Republic of the eighteenth century, a "burgher" was a fully enfranchised citizen with rights to political representation and ownership of property. As the white Boer population expanded over 150 years of occupation, the burghers expropriated the land of the Hottentots in the south and southwest and built their fortunes on Hottentot labor. The Hottentots lived and labored in conditions not dissimilar from those of the slave population (3).

The southern coast of Africa is bordered on the southwest by the Atlantic Ocean and on the southeast by the Indian Ocean.

Within this area are the fertile lands of Cape Town, Port Elizabeth, East London, and Durban (fig. 14).

Map of South Africa (fig. 14)

During this period, before the African independence movements of the twentieth century, various European nations had apportioned most of Africa either by war, treaty, or conquest over the indigenous tribes. They paid scant attention to the customs, cultures, or languages of the indigenous peoples during this apportionment process. They acquired and amalgamated territory based primarily on the resources of the area, the superior military power of the combatants, whether the territory contained strong indigenous tribal forces and the area's perceived suitability to provide expatriate populations with a life better than they enjoyed in Europe (2–3).

Life for immigrants and new settlers was not without hardships and loss. Beyond the fertile valleys and mountains of the Cape Peninsular region lay a vast hinterland of scrub and semidesert known as the karoo or the dry country. Dutch trekboers (farmers who settled in previously uninhabited areas of the country to escape British domination) had spread over the area with their sheep and cattle and lived a rough life in their ox carts or crude dwellings, often clashing with the indigenous people. "Parts of the frontier frequently degenerated into a turmoil of cattle raids and intermittent warfare" (2).

Eventually, the British imposed new laws and restrictions and, at one point in 1811, dispatched troops to help the Boers expel the indigenous Xhosa tribe from their land, the Zuurveld. However, in 1819, the Xhosa retaliated. Ten thousand Xhosa warriors attacked the village of Graham to reclaim their land but were beaten back. This impelled the British government to spend 50,000 pounds, a considerable amount at the time, to transport 4,000 men, women, and children to the area and give each family enough funds to acquire land for farming. These immigrants were chosen from a pool of 80,000 applicants in Britain. They arrived in South Africa in 1820, unaware that their allotted land was in a fiercely disputed area where five wars with locals had previously occurred. Additionally, the land was not as suitable for farming as the government had told them. The British government ended up spending a massive amount to protect the settlers from the displaced Xhosa tribe (3).

In addition to these difficulties, the British administration of the area was faced with the demands of arriving missionaries who took a dim view of slavery and the excessive ill treatment that the Dutch trekboers visited upon the indigenous people.

Consequently, in 1828, "the Cape Authorities promulgated an ordinance making the indigenous Hottentots and other free people of color equal before the law with whites, and removing legal restrictions on their movements" (4). Much to the chagrin of the Dutch settlers, the British government abolished slavery for all their colonies in 1834.

In 1853, the year Alfred Beit was born, a former British colonial secretary, Earl Grey, concluded that "the Government's commitment to British Settlement in Southern Africa...was the most expensive in the annals of the British Empire." Except for the value of the naval facilities on the peninsula, the areas interior of the Southern Cape were described as "the most sterile and worthless in the whole Empire, with no commercial significance" (3).

Then, in 1866, some children playing on a Boer farm at Kimberley discovered a 22-carat diamond near the Orange River in Griqualand West. It was at first considered a single diamond, but then in 1871, an 83.5-carat diamond was found in a well nearby (Albrecht 29). It led to discovery of the world's richest deposit of diamonds in known history. Diamonds worth 50 million pounds were mined in the Kimberley fields between 1871 and 1888 (Albrecht 29). Alfred Beit was eighteen years old at the time and about to learn the diamond trade at his relatives' company in Amsterdam. At this point, the British expropriated the entire territory surrounding Kimberley.

Beit's ancestry and coming of age

In his book *The Will and The Way*, first published in 1937 with coauthor J. G. Lockhart, Sir Alfred Beit, the nephew of our Alfred Beit, explores Beit's heritage. According to Sir Alfred, at the end of the fifteenth century, King Ferdinand of Spain expelled several thousand Sephardic Jews and Muslims from their "prosperous and cultured life." Many went to Portugal but later, in 1496, King Manuel of Portugal did the same and thousands of Jews moved northward. One of these groups settled in Hamburg, a city founded in 809 AD at the mouth of the Elbe River. By this time, seven hundred years after its founding, Hamburg was an important seaport, having won its independence as a city-state against all the rulers of Central Europe. Imbued with this history, Hamburg had a tolerance for refugees, and particularly the Jews migrating from Portugal and Spain. These Sephardic Jews came with nothing except their religious tenets, their education and culture, and their skills in import and export trade, banking, and broking. They established themselves in Hamburg and became the aristocracy of Hamburg Jewry, looking down on later arriving Ashkenazi Jews from Eastern Europe.

Among the first arrival of Sephardic Jews from Portugal was Isaac Beit, who settled on Elb Strasse, Hamburg, about 1750. His son, Marcus Soloman Beit (1732–1810), was a gold and silver refiner. Isaac's two other sons were Abraham and Raphael Solomon Beit, the great-grandfather of "our" Alfred Beit. All three brothers became gold and silver refiners in Hamburg, founding the first establishment of its kind in Germany (Lockhart and Beit 1).

Notwithstanding Sir Alfred Beit's contention that the Beit family were Sephardic Jews, other biographers note possible Ashkenazi roots (Albrecht 13–14).

Alfred Beit was born in Hamburg on February 15, 1853. Coincidentally, Cecil Rhodes was born in the same year. Although Alfred's parents, Seigfriend and Laura Beit, were of Jewish descent, they had converted to Lutheranism shortly after their marriage.

Siegfried, a merchant, belonged to a well-known Hamburg family, although he was not at all wealthy. Laura, on the other hand, was one of several children, many of whom married well, thus providing a large network of family connections for her offspring. She and Seigfriend had six children: three daughters (one older and two younger than Alfred), and three sons (Alfred and his two younger brothers, Theodor and Otto). Siegfried's constant ill health adversely affected his business and reduced his income to an amount barely adequate to meet the needs of the family.

Laura was a remarkable woman, determined to provide every possible educational and social advantage for her children. She taught them how to be frugal with small amounts and this disciplined approach to such expenditures stayed with Alfred all his life, even though he was more freehanded with large expenditures. His lifelong generosity to adversaries, friends and people he scarcely knew was prodigious (Fort 50) (fig. 15).

Beit Family Group, Hamburg, 1880s (fig. 15)

Diminutive in stature (he was only 5'2" tall), Alfred's friends and family nicknamed him "Little Alfred." Educated at the well-known private school of Doctor Schleiden in Hamburg, he was only an average student. In one incident, Alfred decided to impress his parents by telling them that he had moved up to the top of his class, but a few days later, the headmaster himself arrived at the Beit household and debunked Alfred's white lie. This convinced Alfred's father that, unlike his brilliant brother Theodor, who would become a music professor, Alfred's future was not in academics (15).

In 1870, at the age of eighteen, Beit joined Lippert & Co., a woolen company owned by his cousins that dealt in wool and diamonds. However, given the recent discovery of diamonds in South Africa, the Beit family drew on Laura's extensive family connections to arrange an apprenticeship for Alfred with a well-known diamond dealer in Amsterdam, Europe's main center for processing precious stones. After he fulfilled his military obligations in 1874, Alfred went to Amsterdam and began to learn the diamond trade. He apparently dutifully fulfilled his work but without any noticeable ambition or zeal (Albrecht 23–24).

Shortly thereafter, Albert's relatives, the Lipperts, established the Cape Colony branch of D. Lippert & Co., and in September 1875, at the age of twenty-two, Alfred sailed for Cape Town as a representative for the Lippert firm (Albrecht 36). After landing, he had to trek four hundred miles by bullock wagon, sleeping at night on the veldt, to get to the firm's branch in Port Elizabeth and then almost immediately left there, traveling by wagon, for the diamond mining center of Kimberley (fig. 16).

Drawing illustrating typical roads over which
southern African pioneers travelled (fig. 16)

Alfred Beit's journey to Kimberley was the turning point in his life. Whereas he had been a diligent, capable, but disinterested clerk in Amsterdam in 1871, he now became a focused, curious and accomplished diamond buyer. While working in Kimberley, he met Julius Wernher and Cecil Rhodes and, operating through dozens of companies incorporated with them and others, became one of the most powerful mining magnates in history and one of the richest men in Europe.

In *Alfred Beit: A Study of the Man and his Work*, Fort goes to some length to analyze Alfred's character and the keys to his success in both his professional and private life.

> It was because he was so sincere that he was so spontaneous and so seldom self-conscious. It was a quality that stamped itself upon his every action both in the social and the business world, and drew all men to him—British and Dutch, rich and poor, those who gained distinction, and those who could never rise from complete mediocrity. Sincerity seemed, as it were, positively to flow from him. It expressed itself in the radiance of his smile that denied his unalert, dreamy, too solid appearance and revealed the light-hearted spirit within—ever ready, when occasion offered, to cast responsibility aside, and disport itself in an atmosphere of simple gaiety and joyousness… Beit loved simplicity, and retained a child's appreciation of quite simple ordinary things… He became that rather rare product, a self-made but really unselfish millionaire. The proposition is not so simple as it sounds. He had to be a fighter before he could become a philanthropist (Fort 56–57).

An anecdote by one of Beit's colleagues demonstrates Beit's power of concentration and analytic ability. It was the colleague's assignment to explain to Alfred the nature of the business that would be discussed at an upcoming board meeting. The colleague described their discussion as follows:

> To the details involved, there would be no end. One read rapidly, raising one's voice against the traffic, and Mr. Beit had not even read the papers to which they referred. Through the traffic went the brougham, the voice of the reader the while quoting endless and interminable prices, Mr. Beit to all appearances quite inattentive. Half an hour later, at the meeting, Beit would on a sudden arouse himself, and explain with perfect fullness and lucidity, the true inwardness of the situation under discussion, and out of the scrappy information he had apparently not heard, he would elaborate both an exposition and a policy (62).

One of Beit's closest friends and colleagues, J. B. ("Lucky Jim") Taylor wrote the following about Beit in his 1939 memoirs, *A Pioneer Looks Back*:

> One could not help loving the dear man, for he was so perfectly natural and human, and had such a broad outlook on life. He never bore any malice and never said an uncharitable thing about anyone. He had a most unselfish disposition, and was always thoughtful for others. He never forgot a friend. In business, he was a genius, quick to grasp values and take advantage of opportunities. (Taylor 49)

> He was very generous in rewarding anyone who introduced profitable business to him; consequently, most people who had propositions to offer came to him before going to anyone else. (50)

When Beit arrived in Kimberley in 1875 at the young age of 22, the town had been in existence for four years and some semblance of order had been established. The Illicit Diamond Act was in force, and mob and lynch law had been replaced by a Lieutenant Governor and a police force. At the time there were thousands of diggers working their claims on the open fields of the Kimberley, De Beers and Du Toits Pan Mines. In aggregate, they were mining diamonds worth 40,000 to 50,000 pounds a week. As diamond buyer for the Lipperts, Alfred would go from dig to dig to buy the rough stones almost as soon as they came out of the ground. Soon Alfred set up a tent to conduct business, and would have the diggers come to him to sell their product. Beit kept a bag of silver open on the counter in his tent. In exchange for a sovereign's worth of rough stones, he would simply say to the digger, "Help yourself." This gesture of trust went over big with the diggers, and they responded to his trust with scrupulous honesty and respect. (69)

Life in the camps was not all work. Much to the delight and amusement of the diggers and others in camp, Alfred bought the biggest horse he could find, sixteen hands, and tried to learn to ride. Eventually, after much amusement for onlookers, he and his horse, "Captain," adapted to each other, and he went riding early every morning. As his lifelong friend and confidant, Mr. J.B. Taylor, writes, "he was not so proficient on a bike, on which he often crashed into a ditch, to the amusement of everyone." (70)

Although Kimberley had no dancing saloons, Beit did frequent a private club. At twenty-two, he was a good-looking fellow, with brown eyes, dark hair and whiskers. Although short, he would pick the tallest, biggest woman for his dancing partner but, instead of dancing with her, he would gleefully run around her. He became hopelessly mixed up in square dances. This was a time of learning his craft, hands on in the field, having fun, and gaining the respect of the diggers, the mine owners and the everyday people who worked in and around the mining camps. His astute business acumen earned their admiration, trust, and loyalty. (71)

In 1878, at the age of twenty-five, Alfred revisited Hamburg. His earlier Amsterdam training had enabled him to see that South African Cape diamonds, far from deserving their reputation as an inferior product, were generally as good as any in the world, and were being sold in Africa at a price far below their worth in Europe. Accordingly, borrowing £2000 capital from his father, he returned to Kimberley that same year, left Lippert & Co., and set up under his own name as a diamond merchant, determined to amass his own fortune. Foreseeing the growth of Kimberley, he invested most of the capital from his father in purchasing land on which he built a number of corrugated iron offices. For twelve of these, his rental income was estimated at £1800 a month, and much later, he is believed to have sold the land for £260,000 (Auerbach 11).

In 1882, Beit, now twenty-nine, became associated in the diamond business at Kimberley with Julius Porges, a French diamond merchant who had left his lucrative business in Paris for the even more lucrative diamond fields in Kimberley, and Julius Wernher, who became Beit's lifelong friend and partner. By this time, various syndicates and companies had bought out the individual diggers, who had totally disappeared. There was the old De Beers Mining Company, founded by Rhodes in 1880 (Albrecht 48), Du Toits Pan, and Bulfontein. Beit's new associates, Porges & Co., were interested in these companies, and traded them on the stock markets in London and the continent.

However, after a short-lived boom in the market, the oversupply of diamonds overwhelmed demand and many of those connected with the diamond business went bust. According to J. B. Taylor (fig. 17), it was then that the true financial genius of Alfred Beit shifted into high gear. Using loans, Beit transformed many of these companies from insolvency to prosperity, winning friends as well as influence in the companies (Fort 72).

J.B. Taylor-Randlord (fig. 17)

At this point, Beit became convinced that merger of all the diamond interests was the path to riches, and he began to formulate plans to achieve this objective.

Late one night when he was working on this plan, Cecil Rhodes, who was the same age as Beit, looked into his office and remarked: "Hullo. Do you never take a rest?"

"Not often," Beit replied.

"Well, what is your game?" Rhodes asked.

"I am going to control the whole diamond industry before I am much older," said Beit.

Rhodes responded, "That's funny, I have made up my mind to do the same thing. We had better join hands" (Albrecht 48).

Thus began "the Scheme of Amalgamation," the historic pact between Alfred Beit and Cecil Rhodes that "eventually resulted in the creation of De Beers Consolidated Mines Ltd., which practically absorbed all the other companies in Kimberley" (Fort 72–73). The scheme took effect in 1888 after Beit had advanced to Rhodes, without security, a sum of £250,000 so he could buy out all competitors (75). After DeBeers Consolidated Mines was incorporated, Beit became one of five lifetime governors, along with Julius Wernher.

Yielding to the force of Rhodes's personality, Alfred Beit became his intimate friend, accepting his ideas and aspirations with enthusiasm. The two became so close that the question "What would Beit say?" became a regular part of Rhodes's business process (Albrecht 52) (fig. 18).

Cecil Rhodes and Alfred Beit (fig. 18)

CHAPTER 6

Gold In The Rand: 1886–1889

Beit, Rhodes, Wernher, and Taylor become Randlords

In 1886, when Alfred was in his midthirties and by then a very wealthy man, the richest deposit of gold ever was discovered in the Witwatersrand, between Johannesburg and Pretoria, later known as "the Rand." It completely transformed the Transvaal into a boom town (Meredith 174).

Gold mining activity in the Transvaal Republic region of South Africa first began at Barberton in 1884. Most of the prospectors were Brits from Natal and Kimberley, and the Boers looked on them with a mixture of hostility and indifference. With the discovery of the extensive deposit in the Rand, however, the focus changed, and the Rand was declared a public goldfield on 20 September 1886 (Albrecht 65). Early in 1888, Beit paid the Rand a visit, but before leaving Kimberley, he arranged provisionally that a colleague, Hermann Eckstein, should establish a branch of Beit's firm on the Rand, trading as H. Eckstein, later H. Eckstein & Co. (70). Perceiving the gold deposit possibilities of the area, Beit acquired a large interest in the best of the outcrop mines—the mines where gold was visible on the surface. These soon became valuable properties, but Beit's foresight was really in evidence several years later when he revisited South Africa and showed his characteristic perception of possibilities in encouraging the development of slant mining (described below) (193).

Notably, Cecil Rhodes was vehemently opposed to Beit diverting his capital from the diamond industry, in which both Beit and Rhodes were heavily invested, into the gold industry. J. B. Taylor, who agreed with Beit about the financial opportunities that the new discovery offered, recounts in his memoirs, *Lucky Jim*, a sleepy two-hour postmidnight conversation when Rhodes awakened him and proceeded to berate him about the folly of investing in gold in the Rand (Taylor 98). According to Taylor, Rhodes's reluctance stemmed from his fear that Beit would divert the De Beers diamond resources into a losing gold venture which would undercut Rhodes's dreams for expanding his and Britain's political influence in the north (Taylor 96). In *The Life of Jameson*, Ian Colvin also recounts Rhodes's reluctance to invest his diamond fortune into gold. Rhodes was not a gambler, but his friends, Dr. Sauer and J.B. Taylor, persuaded him to at least visit the Rand. After seeing it, Rhodes remarked to Sauer that "When I am in Kimberley [diamond mines in Rhodesia] and I have nothing much to do, I go and sit at the edge of the De Beers Mine, and I look at the blue ground below, and I can calculate the number of loads of blue and the value of the diamonds in the blue and the power these diamonds give me. But this I cannot do with your gold reefs" (Colvin 10).

Rhodes was not alone in his misgivings about South African gold and had good reason to be skeptical about the profitability of the mines. Earlier gold discoveries in the region had fizzled out, and thousands were ruined. Beit and Jules Porges themselves had sold out just in time to avoid the worst of the earlier gold crash in Barberton, but not without loss. London investors lost huge sums, and South African gold shares were viewed with deep distrust (Meredith 174).

Despite their earlier experience, however, Beit and Taylor disagreed with Rhodes, and it was in the Rand that Beit's financial and technical expertise multiplied his fortunes many fold. In the 1890s, some were advocating the use of slant mining, a new method of gold excavation being used in the United States. It involved striking the gold reef by slanting deep level shafts at some distance away from the outcrop. Beit, in the face of much expert skepticism, believed that it might be possible not only to work the gold outcrops but also to mine at a much deeper level. Beit was the first to recognize the importance of employing first-class American mining engineers, and with his capital and their aid, he proved the practicability of slant mining, and his firm became the forerunner in the use of this method of mining. Using his penchant for hands-on management and his unique vision of using slant mining and US mining engineers, Beit was able to exploit the gold potential of the Rand far beyond what other Randlords were able to produce.

Eventually, Beit and Taylor convinced Rhodes that the Rand was "a gold mine," and Rhodes made purchases with C. D. Rudd that became the foundation of one of the chief mining houses on the Rand, the Consolidated Goldfields of South Africa (Fort 100).

In 1884, Porges and Wernher had returned to England and set up the London firm of J. Porges & Co., dealing in diamonds and diamond shares, and after 1888 in gold mines as well. Beit was the sole representative of the firm dealing in diamonds at Kimberley until 1889, when he took up residence in London. Although from then on, London was his headquarters, he continued to visit Africa frequently. On January 1, 1890, Wernher, Beit & Co. replaced J. Porges & Co. in the same lines of business.

CHAPTER 7

The Jameson Raid—Precursor To The Boer War

Beit's disastrous decision and his trial before Parliament

As noted above, the Boers and their leader, Paul Kruger, head of the Transvaal government, didn't pay much attention to the gold-mining activity in the Transvaal in the early 1880s, despite the fact that they were at the time in a quandary as to how to fund the government. However, when word of the discovery of enormous deposits in the Rand reached Kruger, he suddenly saw gold as the way to save the Transvaal from bankruptcy. The British also saw the potential in the area and quickly appropriated it.

Thus, the battle for control of southern Africa was joined between the British, led by Cecil Rhodes, and the Afrikaners, led by Kruger. Rhodes was a ruthless entrepreneur and was in charge of superior British military forces, private and public, as well as enormous financial resources.

The reason why Rhodes, a private citizen, could wield so much power was due to a system the British government used to expand its empire without expending enormous resources in administration. In 1889, Rhodes had incorporated the British South Africa Company ("BSAC"). The British government granted this private organization a Royal Charter, allowing it to acquire land in southern Africa and administer it at its own expense without any cost to the British. The BSAC could employ its own paramilitary police force where local rulers permitted, and could count on British military support against rival European powers or local rebellions. Guaranteed a monopoly, it was permitted to profit commercially by renting out land, receive royalties on mined minerals, levy customs duties, and collect other fees (*Wikipedia*, British South Africa Company, accessed 11/19/20). Private investors funded the company with hope of high financial rewards. The charter gave the company the backing of the British government in its enterprises and allowed the government to expand its sphere of influence in southern and central Africa at no cost. The cynical referred to this as "imperialism on the cheap." Although this charter system was not unusual in the colonial era, the Charter issued to BSAC granted the broadest powers ever given to a private company and with it, BSAC could do virtually anything it wanted (Albrecht 58).

On occasion, BSAC engaged in blatant acts of military conquest and the British exacted tremendous pain and suffering on the Boers by limiting their income from the country's resources. Kruger did not succumb easily, however, despite the decimation of his people. He was a wily politician and the leader of his people in the Boer War against the British, fought from 1899 to 1902.

The war had been presaged in 1895 by a notorious raid against the Afrikaners instigated by Rhodes, whose main goal was expanding the extent and influence of the British empire. He was joined in the conspiracy by Starr Jameson and other entrepreneurs intent on gaining total control and governance of all of Southern Africa for the British. Other Randlords, including Alfred Beit, financed the effort. The raid failed, however, because Jameson disobeyed orders and rode into the Transvaal without waiting for sufficient military support, leading to an ignominious defeat for the English-speaking conspirators and an international crisis. The raid was denounced in the embarrassed British House of Commons, which wanted nothing more than to distance itself from the venture and to avoid the blame for its failure. In 1896, the House of Commons held a parliamentary inquiry on the raid spearheaded by Liberal MP William Harcourt, which implicated both Rhodes and Beit. There was disastrous publicity by the press led by the infamous columnist Labouchere, publisher of a magazine called *Truth,* and a major foe of Beit and Rhodes (fig. 19).

MORE LABOUCHERE CHARGES.

Alfred Beit Demands a Retraction in the Transvaal Raid Inquiry.

LONDON, May 28.—There was another scene to-day in the Committee Room off Westminster Hall, during the examination of Mr. Alfred Beit, a former Director of the British Chartered South Africa Company, before the Parliamentary Committee appointed to inquire into the Transvail raid. Mr. Beit demanded that Mr. Henry Labouchère should either prove or withdraw the charges he had made against him, the witness, in Truth. Thereupon Mr. Labouchère proceeded to question the former Director regarding transactions on the Stock Exchange, saying:

" Do you challenge me on this? "

" I challenge you on your vile attacks on me," retorted Mr. Beit.

" Then I will prove them," replied Mr. Labouchère.

The Chairman, Mr. William L. Jackson, pointed out that Mr. Labouchère himself had withdrawn the charges referred to. Mr. Labouchère, however, persisted in saying he had not done so.

On motion of Mr. Joseph Chamberlain, the Secretary of State for the Colonies, the Committee Room was then cleared.

The committee afterward adjourned.

The New York Times
Published: May 29, 1897
Copyright © The New York Times

Labouchere Charges against Beit concerning the Jameson Raid (fig. 19)

Labouchere and Harcourt used the raid to showcase their criticism of the entire Charter system of imperialism and in particular the fact that a private company (BSAC) was indirectly exercising state power under a Royal Charter granted by the British government (Albrecht 80). Labouchere's public denunciation of the self-effacing Beit, who always did his best to maintain a low public profile, was devastating. At the end of the inquiry in 1897, the House of Commons censured Rhodes and Beit. Rhodes's political career was ruined and he was forced to give up his position as premier of the Cape Colony and Chairman of BSAC and Beit was forced to resign as one of its directors (Albrecht 81).

By this time, the late 1890s, Alfred Beit was one of the richest men in Europe. His knowledge and astute development of diamonds in South Africa at the Kimberley Mines had laid the financial groundwork for his expanding empire into the goldfields of the Rand. He held a lifelong position as a director in De Beers Consolidated Mines Ltd. His company, Wernher, Beit & Co., became, after De Beers, his second most important source of wealth, making him one of the richest Randlords (Albrecht 67). He had established himself on 26 Park Place Lane in London, would soon lease the Hertfordshire Estate of Lord Cowper, Tewin Water, and was moving among the elite in the highest social circles of British society. He was still only in his forties, but his many years of pushing himself beyond his endurance in South Africa had taken a toll on his health, and his harsh interrogation before the House of Commons left him in a state of depression. The trial ended in 1897, and Beit, embarrassed and crestfallen by the diminishment of his heretofore unblemished personal integrity, was ready for a period of relaxation, travel, and cultural enrichment.

CHAPTER 8

Escape Overseas In the Yacht *Iolaire*

Cruising the world

After his censure by the House of Commons, Beit decided to escape from the public eye. He commissioned Sir Donald Currie's yacht, *Iolaire*, and gathered up his friends Lucky Jim Taylor, Starr Jameson (fig. 20), Henri Robinow (his cousin), and a few others and made plans for a three-month cruise in the refurbished yacht for various ports of call (Albrecht 118) (fig. 21). They had no stated specific timetable or destination. They were determined, now that they had each achieved enormous wealth, to visit various parts of the world, to see the art of France and the cities of Germany and other European countries, Egypt, and wherever their fancy led them. After all, they had a seventy-foot, well-equipped and stocked yacht, with a competent crew, and time to get away from it all. Cecil Rhodes joined the yacht at Naples on the return.

Dr. Starr Jameson (fig. 20)

The Wanderers' Club, South Africa, 1889. Hermann Eckstein
and J.B. Taylor are seated in the center. (fig. 21)

The exact date of Beit's departure from England after mid-1897
on the *Iolaire* is unclear, but we know some of the exotic places where
he docked. When the group set sail at Marseilles, it proceeded to

Monte Carlo, Corsica, Naples, Tunis, Algiers, and then to Malta, Alexandria, Athens, Cyprus and Crete, Constantinople, the Black Sea, and the Adriatic Sea (Albrecht 118; Taylor 176). The group went up the Nile as far as Assouan and finally sailed for Jaffa where they left the yacht and went on tour through Palestine (Taylor 175, 176). It was during this foray that Beit acquired many of his art treasures. Despite the admonishment of his friends to relax, the cruise did not stop Beit from sending telegrams and letters from various ports of call to keep up with his empire of business interests.

In October 1899, five months after my mother's birth, Beit was back in Europe, traveling to Berlin (App. 1). From then until his death, Beit continued travelling frequently to South Africa and managing his extensive business affairs. In 1903, he was again invited to and joined the board of BSAC (Taylor 184). Even after suffering a collapse in Rhodesia in 1903, he again "threw himself vehemently into the work of daily life" (Taylor 182–186) until his declining health made it impossible for him to continue.

Alfred Beit's net worth at the time of his death at Tewin Water in 1906 was over £8,000,000. The entity he founded with Rhodes, De Beers Consolidated Mines Ltd., remains today as one of the most powerful diamond and gold companies in the world. During his lifetime and in his will, Beit donated enormous sums of money and works of art to multiple German museums and endowed universities, medical institutions, and research facilities, including the University of Hamburg. The Beit Trust, created with £1,200,000, was unique in that it was expressly purposed to promote an underdeveloped country (Albrecht 122). In addition to schools and other facilities in South Africa, the Trust had built more than forty bridges by 1932, of which the Alfred Beit Bridge, crossing the Limpopo River between Mussina and Beitbridge, is but one (Albrecht 125).

CHAPTER 9

Tewin Water

Beit's "Downton Abbey" and our newfound friends

I have always been fascinated with Tewin Water, the country manor house and vast estate where Alfred spent his last days, and the small churchyard where he, his brother Otto, and Otto's wife are buried. I felt that the house and local records might contain correspondence that would reveal Alfred's whereabouts between mid-1897 and 1899. Was he in British Guiana during that period, the period when diamonds were discovered in the interior and where Wernher, Beit & Co. purchased a mining lease on substantial acreage? He had always been a hands-on manager, and with De Beers and Wernher, Beit had always been keen to control the diamond supply, if not to suppress it.

So on March 17, 2012, Anita, our friend Dr. Lena Chang, and I set off on a second trip to England to explore its records of British history and lore.

We stayed at Lena's timeshare townhouse on Sloane Square, twenty yards from the tube. It became our staging area for visits to three British Archives in search of information: The National Archives at Kew Gardens; the Derbyshire Records Office in Matlock, Derbyshire; and the Hertfordshire Records Office, and finally, for Tewin Water, Selwyn, Hertfordshire, in the Mimram River valley, the site of Beit's country estate. With Rod Leggetter and his wife, current residents of the Beit mansion (now a condominium), we shared a memorable tea and a tour that impressed us with how the essential aspects of Beit's mansion had been preserved (fig. 22, 23). Although Rod told us that there were no original Beit documents left in the mansion when he acquired ownership, there was one picture on his wall that interested me. It was a turn-of-the-century picture of about twenty of Alfred Beit's household staff, including the head of the staff, dressed more formally than the others. Rod had gotten the picture from his daughter-in-law, whose grandfather had been this very same head of staff at Tewin Water. What secrets could he have revealed? I still hadn't uncovered the secret of my grandfather's identity.

Beit's Tewin Water Mansion as restored, 2014 (fig. 22)

Interior of Tewin Water mansion as restored. (fig. 23)

As noted above, by 1897, Alfred Beit was beginning to move in the social circles of the English elite. He and many of the other Randlords (those *nouveau riche* who made fortunes from the gold mines of the Rand area of South Africa) maintained houses in London, but Beit was the only Randlord invited to the Duchess of Devonshire's June, 1897 Jubilee Costume Ball, one of the top social events in Britain (Albrecht 102). He attended dressed in the costume of a Stadhouder of Holland (fig. 24). Interestingly, the Duchess who threw that costume ball in 1897 was at the time the mother-in-law of the future Duchess of Devonshire, Deborah Mitford Cavendish, whom I had recently met in New York.

Alfred Beit at the Duchess of Devonshire's Jubilee Ball,
dressed as a Dutch Stadhouder, 1897 (fig. 24)

Beit also received invitations from the Prince of Wales (later King Edward VII) to visit Sandringham (Albrecht 102), was building a house on Park Lane in London (Albrecht 90) (fig. 25), and would soon acquire a long-term lease for Tewin Water, where he would entertain friends and enjoy the fishing and partridge shooting on the estate.

Alfred Beit's House, Park Lane, London (fig. 25)

Tewin Water is one of those beautiful rural communities in England whose history dates back to the Anglo-Saxon era from AD 410–800. Its ruling dynasty was established in the early sixth century.

St. Peter's Church, where Alfred and his brother, Otto, are buried is prominent in the community and has been used continuously for worship for 1,300 years (fig. 26). Its history begins with the coming of the Saxons in AD 449, who worshipped the god Tew, the Saxon god of war, from which Tewin Water received its name. The site of Tew's shrine became that of a Christian Church after the Saxons converted to Christianity in or about AD 604 (*The People of Tewin* 51).

Sir Otto Beit, Alfred Beit's brother (fig. 26)

In addition to holding the remains of Alfred Beit, Sir Otto, and his wife, and Theodor (fig. 27), the graveyard is the burial site of John and Geoffrey de Havilland of de Havilland aircraft fame and their mother, Lady Louise de Havilland, who died in 1949 at the age of 70. Although the family did not live in Tewin, their famous de Havilland airplane factory was located not far away in Hatfield (62).

Gravesite of Alfred, Theodor and Sir Otto Beit (fig. 27)

After the Leggetters took us to Beit's gravesite, we went into the church where, coincidentally, Rod's daughter was married. There we saw a plaque dedicated to Theodor Beit, Sir Otto's son, who was named after Otto and Alfred's brother, Theodor (fig. 28).

Plaque memorializing Theodor Beit, Alfred Beit's nephew (fig. 28)

The Tewin Water estate was owned from the thirteenth century until the Dissolution of the Monasteries in 1540 by the Priory of St. Bartholomew, Smithfield. In 1544, it was in the ownership of Sir Thomas and Mary Wrothe and their family. In 1620, the manor was sold and for a time became the property of the second Earl of Salisbury and eventually descended to his son. In 1689, a new owner, James Fleet, built the first house on the property. Fleet's father, a wealthy merchant, became Lord Mayor in 1692. Upon Fleet's death in 1733, his widow, Lady Elizabeth Cathcart, inherited the estate and house. Lady Cathcart was a great beauty who ended up with three more husbands. On her last wedding ring was inscribed: "If I survive, I'll make it to five." Her fourth and final marriage, however, brought her great grief and misery. Her fourth husband, Hugh Maguire, was a forty-year-old Irish adventurer, commonly known as the "wicked colonel." Lady Elizabeth was fifty-four at the time of their marriage, and Maguire became notorious for his appalling treatment of her, terrorizing her in an effort to get her to hand over her jewels and the deed to Tewin Water House. She refused to do so and, in retaliation, he kidnapped her and spirited her off to his family home in Ireland, where she remained his prisoner for twenty-one years (95–96).

After Maguire's death, Lady Elizabeth returned to Tewin Water, where she lived for another twenty-one years, dying in 1789 at the age of ninety-eight. She was buried with her first husband, James Fleet, in St. Peter's Churchyard. By that time, the third Earl of Cowper had bought the house to cover mortgages. The Earl also died in 1789; the house was demolished, and a new one built in its place. In 1798 Henry Cowper, the fifth Earl of Cowper, clerk of the House of Lords, demolished the new house and commissioned John Groves to design a house in the then-fashionable neo-Greek style. Humphrey Repton designed the landscaping. After Henry Cowper's death in 1840, Tewin Water House boasted a number of distinguished tenants, including Mr. John Currie from 1856 to 1861 and Mr. Herbert Arthur Trower from 1892 to 1902. In 1902, Alfred Beit acquired the house on a long-term lease and from then until 1950, it was the country retreat of the Beit family. In 1906, Sir

Otto (Beit's brother) was able to buy the property from the Cowper family heirs (99).

Sir Otto and Lillian Beit had two sons and two daughters. Their eldest son, Theodor, whose memorial plaque we had seen in the church, entered the army during World War I and became a Second Lieutenant. In 1930, at the tender age of eighteen, believing that his fellow officers were snubbing him, he wrote a heartbreaking letter to his family and took his own life. Sir Otto's second son, Alfred Beit, inherited Tewin Water House and the Baronetcy upon Sir Otto's death and Otto's wife, Lady Lillian, continued to live there. During World War II, Alfred was commissioned in the RAF, and in 1939, he married Clementine Mitford, a cousin of the celebrated (and at time infamous) Mitford sisters (100).

Among the eminent people who visited Tewin Water House during its heyday were many film stars, including Greta Garbo and General Charles De Gaulle, who stayed for many months as Lady Lillian Beit's guest during World War II. In 1945, Lady Lillian left Tewin Water and moved to her London home in Belgravia. Subsequently the house and grounds became a country club and, later, a school for children with hearing problems. The school was relocated in 1997 and the remaining 1,000 acres were sold. The mansion fell into disrepair until, in 2000, it was renovated to its former glory and subdivided into privately owned condominiums (103).

Since our 2012 trip to Tewin Water, we have visited with Rod and Jan Leggetter and their Scottish friends, Sandy and Cathy Black (proud Scots with the delightful Scottish brogue), many times. They have become good friends, and have visited and played golf with us in the US, and we have visited and played golf with them several times and spent many memorable evenings together near Tewin Water. We enjoyed one delightful week with the four of them at the Black's vacation home on Lake Annecy in France. Thus, whether or not our search for my grandfather is successful, it led us to four dear friends whom we cherish (fig. 29).

Chris, Anita, and Rod and Jan Leggetter at Brockett Hall,
Welwyn, Garden City, Hertfordshire (fig. 29)

CHAPTER 10

DNA And Other Clues

Honing in

Since we are both engineers, Tony and I approached the search for Grandpa analytically. However, we unwittingly approached it from two separate perspectives. Tony postulated that Alfred Beit was not our grandfather, and he went about trying to prove that postulate. He created a timeline (App. 1) using his and my research data to show Alfred's whereabouts from birth to death. No trivial detail escaped Tony's systematic study. For example, he found that on February 5, 1898, not long after Beit's disastrous censure by the British House of Commons, the *New York Times* reported that the wedding of Alfred Beit to Mary Moore would soon be announced. Moore was an actress, the daughter of parliamentary agent Charles Moore, and the widow of one James Alberry. As it turned out, the wedding did not take place.

This was not the first time that Beit had left a hopeful at the altar. In January 1888, Beit had an illegitimate daughter named Olga (called "Queenie") with Mrs. Elizabeth Bennett of Kimberley, South Africa (Albrecht 93). In 1890, as reported in *The New York Times* on July 16, 1906, Beit took out an insurance policy with the Equitable Life Insurance Society in the US, which included $70,000 (US) for the same Elizabeth Bennett, "my intended wife" (and, coincidentally, the mother of his child). However, they never married.

On March 30, 1898, Alfred Beit was granted British citizenship from the British Home Office in London. (Albrecht 136). On September 25, 1899, four months after Mummy's birth, Alfred met with a Major Leonard in South Africa to discuss possible new gold discoveries. But where was Alfred in the interim, between July and September of 1898 when Mummy was conceived?

One clue was the information I found in one of my visits to the British National Archives in Kew Gardens, mentioned above. The entry, in volume 5 of the 1902 *British Guiana Journal*, indicated that Wernher, Beit & Co. had been prospecting in British Guiana before 1902 (fig. 30, 31, 32). The passage followed lengthy discussions about the "scheme" for awarding leases to various entities for precious metal exploration based on criteria such as demonstrated financial capability, size of the land offerings for each lease, and prospects of success for each lease.

Colonial Office Record Book, British Guiana, 1900
(British National Archives) (fig. 30)

British Guiana Register, Colonial Office Records, 1897-1900 (fig. 31)

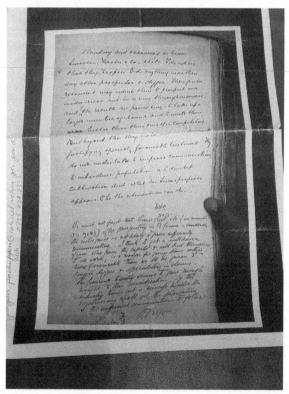

Entry from Colonial Office Record book referencing Wernher,
Beit & Co. in British Guiana before 1902 (fig. 32)

The entry intrigued me for a variety of reasons. First, it definitely established that Wernher, Beit had been in British Guiana looking for diamonds in the years before 1902. Previous references I read in *The New York Times* and other contemporary sources had referred to the interested British Guiana Syndicate as "De Beers," but this entry gave me proof that not one, but two, of Alfred Beit's companies were engaged there in the crucial years. In addition, I knew that Alfred Beit had instructed Wernher to destroy some of his personal correspondence after his death (Albrecht 137). It would seem logical that if Alfred had been in British Guiana, as seems likely from the *1902 British Foreign Office Journal*, and if he had had an affair there that resulted in the birth of a child, he, an intensely private person, would have wanted to keep the affair a secret from business colleagues, family, and the British press. Who better to accomplish this end than his friend and business associate in the British Guiana venture, Julius Wernher?

An article in the *The Morning Post*, September 22, 1898, describing Wernher, Beit's contribution for hurricane relief in the West Indies provides still further evidence of Beit's interest in and possible presence in the Caribbean in that year.

Another article in *The New York Times* reference further established an active diamond industry in British Guiana in 1900:

> Big Diamond Find in British Guiana
> St. Thomas, DWI
> April 14, [1900]
>
> According to news received here to-day, the largest find of diamonds in Demerara County, British Guiana, since the diamond industry was started there, has been made on the property of the syndicate. (*The New York Times*, January 12, 1901.)

Then there is the question of DNA, which, if comparative samples could be procured, would be dispositive. There are some clues, however, which point to a possible Beit/Pollard-Martin DNA connection based on what we learned from my DNA and about Alfred Beit's roots.

A June 8, 2015, e-mail from my brother Tony about my own DNA explains:

> Chris,
>
> Your DNA test done in March 2008 stated that you belong to Haplogroup R1b (M269). An Internet search for meaningful attributes of same led me to a web site that offers a scholarly treatment of the subject, and it contained the following paragraph:
>
> 'Two particular TaqI 49a, f haplotypes have been found to be associated with what we now know to be haplogroup R1b1a2. The two haplotypes are ht15 and ht35. ht15 is most commonly found in western European R1b1a2, and most likely represents a Mesolithic or Neolithic population expansion in Western Europe. ht35, the parent haplotype of ht15, is most commonly found in southeastern Europe and southwestern Asia. Elevated levels of ht35 have also been observed among Ashkenazi and Sephardic Jewish populations.'
>
> The search continues, unabated.
>
> Tony

Thus, it is fair to infer that my DNA, which reveals Ashkenazi and Sephardic Jewish origins, comports with the Beit family's origins and history dating back to the 1570s and probably before. Beit family DNA would definitively establish the relationship.

During my research, friends would give me many pictures of British Guiana during the 1890s and 1900s—pictures of people, beautiful colonial buildings, and local scenes. One such picture that appeared in a railroad publication from British Guiana ca. 1900 particularly caught my eye (fig. 33). It shows a tram, recently delivered, standing in front of which are several well-dressed men in different forms of attire. A second photo in a contemporaneous Georgetown publication shows a piece of railroad equipment accompanied by a sign reading "Steam Sleigh, Cecil Rhodes"(fig. 34). This is not surprising because Rhodes and Beit had long recognized that rail transportation was intrinsic to their business interests.

Photo of new tram in Georgetown showing three men who appear to be J.B. Taylor, Starr Jameson, and Alfred Beit (fig. 33)

101 Steam Winch for kanting Greenheart on Sproston's Timber grants, Demerara

Photo of Steam Sleigh in Georgetown, Demerara County, British Guiana identifying Cecil Rhodes as the supplier, early 1900s (fig. 34)

Rhodes and Beit had formed a partnership to fulfill their common dream to build a railroad in Africa from the Cape in South Africa to Cairo, Egypt, in the north of the African continent. A major bridge, the Alfred Beit Bridge, which crosses the Limpopo River between the Transvaal and Rhodesia in Africa, is testament to Beit's interest in transportation in Africa. In his will, he dedicated a large share of his fortune to "The Beit Trust," which he specifically established to engage in the expansion of rail and telecommunication networks in South Africa (Albrecht 122). *The Will and The Way* is, by its own title, "An account of Alfred Beit and the trust which he founded."

When I saw the Guianese tram photo, I looked closely, paying particular attention to the three individuals who stood together. They bore an uncanny resemblance to J. B. Taylor (Lucky Jim), Alfred Beit, and Dr. Starr Jameson, close friends who were on the extended *Iolaire* cruise in 1898. If I am correct, this photo places Beit in British Guiana during the approximate period of the conception and birth of my mother.

CHAPTER 11

Ruby, Her Life, Our Family

"I did it for my children"

Ruby

Ruby Pollard circa 1925

Ruby Pollard ca. 1925 (fig. 35)

Tony, Claire, and I know very little about Mummy's childhood, except that she told Claire that her stepfather was very good to her. During her teenage years, she was "adopted" in Georgetown by a Mrs. Jane Jordan, reputed to be an American from Baltimore, who took her on as an apprentice and taught her the art of cooking and the business of catering (fig. 35).

It is not exactly clear how Mrs. Jordan became involved in Mummy's life. We have little information about her except that Mummy told Claire that Mrs. Jordan knew all the "moneyed" people and was the caterer for all their entertainment. She also reputedly had a connection of some sort with people in the gold and diamond syndicates.

In any event, Ruby became especially adept in catering. She especially excelled in the art of food presentation and cake decoration. She designed many a friend's wedding cake, including her own. At an early age, she became the first person of color to assume the prestigious position of head housekeeper at Government House, the residence and offices of the British colonial governor of British Guiana and his staff (fig. 36).

Government House, Georgetown (fig. 36)

The job entailed the supervision of all the staff responsible for the functioning of Government House, including state dinners and cocktail parties for the many dignitaries and foreign representatives who were entertained there, as well the upkeep of the building. In 1932 she was running the Tower Hotel, and upon the governor's recommendation, she became a principal instructor at the Carnegie Trade Center, a training school for the culinary and domestic arts. The school had five other principals, four English and one Dutch, but Ruby had the largest staff. Again, she was the first person of color to hold such a responsible position.

It was at Government House that Ruby honed her management and interpersonal skills, and she became a renowned caterer and businessperson. She worked hard at her catering business, but she loved it, and she treated those who worked for her with caring and extreme kindness. After marrying Bertie in her late thirties and giving birth to us three children within four years (fig. 37, 38, 39, 40), she continued to run her catering business from home, supplementing Bertie's income to a significant degree until her sixties (fig. 41). She used her considerable influence and modest earnings to get all of us into private secondary Jesuit and Carmelite Catholic schools, ensuring us a first class British education.

Bertie ca. 1937 (fig. 37)

Ruby ca. 1925 (fig. 38)

Claire and Christopher ca. 1939 (fig. 39)

Christopher and Tony ca. 1947 (fig. 40)

95 New Garden & Robb Streets
Georgetown,
8th June.1956.

The Y.M.C.A. Georgetown
        To Mrs Ruby Martin   .... Dr

TO	Catering as agreed, that is, supplying 4 meals daily for forty (40) seminar students for 40 days, i.e. from 23rd April, 1956 to 2nd June, 1956, at the agreed rate of $2.25 per person per day ..	$ 3,600. 00
	LESS five weekly payments made amounting to	3,000. 00
	BALANCE DUE	$ 600. 00

One of Ruby's catering invoices (fig. 41)

Everyone knew, respected, and loved "Auntie Ruby," as her friends' children called her. Her customers adored her, as did Claire's many school girl friends. They often dropped by after school to say hello to Auntie Ruby, who they knew had finished catering a lawn party or some other major event and would have leftover delicacies like pine tarts, devilled eggs, or her famous eclairs.

"Auntie Ruby, you got any of those eclairs left?"

"Yes, children. Look on the dining table and help yourselves. Meigan, how are things going at home?"

When we asked Mummy at the end of her life why she had worked so long and so hard with little respite, she replied emphatically, "I did it for my children."

Ruby and Bertie

Sometime in the early 1930s, Alexander Adolphus Donovan Martin met the then-engaged Ruby Pollard, a woman six years his senior and an accomplished and successful businesswoman. He was handsome, dark skinned, opinionated, and rising up in the civil service. She was fair skinned, well rounded in appearance, kind, pretty,

89

and at ease in male and female company. They met at a birthday party for a Dr. Carrington, and Ruby was talking to Uncle Cecil Holmes whom Bertie had asked to introduce him to Ruby.

He asked her to dance, and she told him, "I don't want to know anything about you."

After he asked her to go with him to the Seawall, a frequent lover's venue, she said, "No, I'm engaged to someone else."

Not one to give up easily, Bertie pursued her with the same intensity he pursued everything, and in 1936 they were married in the Catholic church (fig. 42). Ruby was thirty-seven, and Bertie was thirty-one. Ruby herself made and decorated their two-tiered wedding cake (fig. 43). Claire was born that same year. We two boys, Christopher and Anthony, followed in 1937 and 1939 (fig. 44).

Bertie and Ruby in Canada, ca. 1947 (fig. 42)

The wedding cake Ruby made for her wedding to Bertie, 1935 (fig. 43)

Bertie, Ruby, and family, Georgetown Botanical
Gardens, ca. 1950 (fig. 44)

Following successful productions of the British plays *To The Lovely Margaret, A Marriage Has Been Arranged* and Terrence Rattigan's *While the Sun Shines* (fig. 45), Bertie was awarded a British Council Scholarship to study drama in the United Kingdom from 1951 to 1952 at the Bristol Old Vic Theatre, founded in 1946 by the famed British actor Sir Lawrence Olivier. During this one-year paid sabbatical from his civil-service job, Mommy and the three of us stayed in British Guiana. While overseas, Daddy visited other parts of Europe, including France (fig. 46, 47). He is remembered for having produced a Commonwealth pageant in London to mark the coronation celebrations of Queen Elizabeth II (Banham, Hill, and Woodyard 192). This exposure to Western European life and culture further enhanced his air of superiority and his fidelity to British drama.

Cast of one of the plays Bertie directed (fig. 45)

Bertie lunching with friends in Montmarte, France, ca. 1951 (fig. 46)

Bertie in Cannes, France, ca. 1951 (fig. 47)

As Claire wrote in her book *When We Were Growing Up in the Land of the Mighty Roraima:*

> Our Dad was a highly intelligent man of strong opinions. He was also an anglophile who, contrariwise, battled against the British colonial rules and their stereotypical (low) expectations of the local population. He constantly challenged these expectations and suffered for it. (Martin 16)

Perhaps Daddy's signature contribution to the Guyanese culture was cofounding the Theatre Guild of Guyana in 1957, where he produced and directed plays for the stage and radio. He also trained actors and was a riveting speaker. Ever the anglophile, however, he did exhibit some disdain for what he felt were inferior West Indian playwrights. In January 1959, Richard Allsop starred in Daddy's production of Lillian Hellman's play *Watch on the Rhine.* Frank Thomasson, in his book *A History of Theatre in Guyana, 1800–2000*, discusses Daddy's significant role in the development of theater in British Guiana and reprints a lengthy tribute to him by Allsop, in which Allsop writes (in part):

> His criticism of local theatre was, in part, our weakness for fine elaborate settings "with too little energy and care spent on getting the acting participants up to a really high standard". This latter anxiety absorbed him and he never presented a costume or period play". The play is the thing, not the fancy setting," he said…
>
> Unfortunately he had little use for the West Indian plays, for being "not yet great," and he would dull his big expressive eyes in mild contempt, not even bothering perhaps to answer, at the mention of local dialect plays. Wrongly perhaps, he concerned himself only with the material of proved and tried quality, and presented in language of more traditional dignity. (Thomasson 128)

In the never-ending dispute among devotees of British Guianese theater concerning the standards that should be applied to theatrical criticism, Daddy's own words epitomize his values and his views. After explaining that the role of a critic is to assess the merits of a production against the background of his own knowledge and experience in dramatic interpretation and expression, he wrote:

> [The critic's purpose] should not be one of compromise with prevailing circumstances or conventions... The idea, implicit in the not infrequent attacks upon the critic, that he should temper his criticism for reasons extraneous to pure assessment is a repugnant one. (Thomasson 250)

That Daddy held these somewhat elitist views is not surprising because, as I have mentioned, the poet Egbert Martin was a great inspiration to him, and Egbert's use of language was quintessentially Victorian English.

Bertie and Ruby's marriage—at once tempestuous, loving, and argumentative—was nonetheless mutually devoted to the education and upbringing of their three children. Their marriage endured until Bertie's death in 1959.

From our infancy, Mummy and Daddy both drilled into us the necessity of a university education and even the professional course each would pursue. Anything less was not an option. To their credit, we all attended Howard University and became successful professionals in the United States, where we prospered and still reside. Claire became a health-care professional, while Tony and I both enjoyed lengthy careers as engineers, all as our parents had prescribed.

Claire

Claire was Daddy's pet. He always insisted that Tony and I escort her to parties on our bikes and return home riding behind her and her boyfriend *du jour*, Rudy or Bull or the short-lived Warren guy. The picture of us with our nanny and a host of other costumed five-year-olds shows how pretty she was (fig. 48, 49, 50).

Claire, Chris and Tony dressed for a costume party ca. 1941 (fig. 48)

Chris dressed for a costume party ca. 1941 (fig. 49)

Chris, Claire and their Nanny (far left partially hidden) at a
costume party ca. 1941 at the Kranenberg's (fig. 50)

That angelic face and demeanor of mine stayed with me through high school and my stint as an altar boy (fig. 51). Claire stayed pretty all her life. Because math was her Achilles' heel, Tony and I used to refer to her contemptuously as the "pretty dummy." Mummy spared no expense to dress her in beautifully colored flared-out dresses, pretty socks embroidered with lace, and patent leather shoes with leather straps with brass buckles. Often when I see a bright lime or orange fabric in a children's store, my mind flashes back to our childhood and the image of Claire at eight years old. She was our sister, and we adored her.

As he did with all of us, Daddy mandated Claire's profession. He told her at any early age that she would be a physical therapist. He recognized her abhorrence of advanced math and her penchant for biology and chemistry at Ursuline College, a Roman Catholic all-girls high school, with high walls around the entire perimeter. Boys did not enter there, and the nuns saw to that. Despite my best efforts, I was never able to see what was inside the wall that hid the "Vestal Virgins," as Tony and I called Claire and her classmates (fig. 52).

Claire and Chris ca. 1942 (fig. 51)

The "Vestal Virgins," Claire's 1954 St. Rose's Catholic High
School graduating class. Claire 3rd from right. (fig. 52)

Well, the "dummy" went on to have a distinguished career in
the health-care field and amass more academic success than Tony or
I did. She ended up with degrees from Howard University (biology),
Columbia University (physical therapy and hospital administration),
and The Wharton School (HMO administration) (fig. 53).

Claire ca. 1985 (fig. 53)

Claire's many health-care administrative assignments with the Red Cross took her to Cleveland, Ohio; Detroit, Michigan; Albany, New York, and finally to Washington, DC, with the Points of Light Foundation. In 1994, she traveled to Russia where she consulted with the Russian Volunteer Movement. In 1999, she coauthored and published her research about the quality of life of older Black women in the *Journal of Gerontological Social Work*. In 2002, she founded the Neuse-Pamlico Sound Women's Coalition in New Bern, North Carolina. She was a member of the New Bern Planning Board, AKA Sorority, and the Links of New York.

In October 14, 1988, the *Schenectady Gazette* featured Claire in a lengthy article on "The Professional Woman." Greta Petry, the reporter, described her as follows:

> Claire P. Martin has that pure professional demeanor that makes you wonder at first if she is for real. Did she rise smoothly to the top? Did adversity ever get in her way? Who is this woman and why did she know exactly what her career goals were? After listening to her story, one realizes that nothing was handed to her. That she made her own way in the world and that she did indeed face obstacles. The serene, in control image she conveys appears to come from the sense of security her parents gave her, and the strength she has gained from confronting difficulty and overcoming it. (Petry)

Claire's answer to the interviewer was quintessentially Claire:

> If I met roadblocks, which there were, I just made a detour and got back on my road… This is a great time in my life. I know what I know, and I know what I don't know and it's OK… I attribute part of my success to the guidance of my parents.

Claire spoke for all three of us. As Black immigrants, we never accepted the conventional wisdom of our "proper" limited role in American society. We used our intellect and education to go around obstacles, and we each achieved success in our lives and leadership in our professions and our communities. Our parents and our grandparents would have been proud of us. You, too, Alfred.

Claire came to the US in 1955 and was married twice. Her first husband, Fred Goldson, was a Jamaican she met there while on vacation and divorced soon after. Then, from 1994 until she passed away in 2011, she was married to the love of her life, Sam Combs of New Bern, North Carolina. Claire never had children of her own.

Anthony (in his own words)

My older brother, Christopher, and I went to Saint Stanislaus College—an advanced high school known as "Saints" for short. Prior to that, we went (with our sister) to a gender-separated primary school called Sacred Heart Roman Catholic School. Let me tell you that the education we received, and that others received at similarly rigorous schools, was as good as the planet had to offer. I know so because many of our peers and many of those that came before us went on to achieve worldwide distinction. I am still trying to figure out how an otherwise "laid-back" culture developed such a fierce scholastic ethic. Could it be that the Colonial British, having solved their labor shortage through indenture, decided that they also needed local brainpower to help run their empire? Alas, the white-collar commute from England could not be sustained. That may be the "why", but what is the "how"?

Part of the "how" may have been mostly unplanned and spontaneous. I believe that over time we fell in love with the British and things British, due to a Stockholm syndrome effect. So how do you learn to emulate the British? The operative word here is *learn*, and you learn through education. Of course, the British, never ones to miss an opportunity, sent some of their best and brightest to fulfill this yearning…enter the Jesuits and their ilk. The Jesuits are the teaching arm of the Catholic Church and to them teaching is not merely a profession, it is a Godly mission…and they are awesome at it!

I am in my first physics class at Saints, the instructor is Father Feeney, and electricity is in the air because physics was our Holy Grail of higher education. My older brother, Chris, prepped me somewhat for this occasion, but I still feel somewhat overwhelmed. To test the mettle of his freshman physics class, Father asks, "How come our bodies are not crushed by the atmosphere's 14.7 pounds per square inch of pressure." All eyes turn first to bright boy Freddy Campayne "because our bodies, through evolution, are built to withstand the pressure."

"Wrong!"

Others tried. Wrong, wrong, wrong! Then, in a moment of clarity that gives me goose bumps to this day, I say, "Because there is an equal and opposite pressure within us pushing out."

"Cooorrreeect! Thank you, Chris!"

I think I recall an ovation. I could sense that I was being reevaluated by my peers. This was a very powerful and inspirational moment for me…I had bested Freddy. Such was the lure of academic achievement and may be part of the "how" mentioned above. Of course, I eventually lapsed into my status of above average mediocrity, but because of Saints, I was still at a respectable place on the academic food chain.

Freddy was a star. His full name was Frederick Campayne. I believe one or both his parents were academics, and he was Black like me. Everybody loved Freddy; he was academically gifted without being nerdy, and in every other regard he was just a nice, regular lad.

Freddy's range of academic excellence was breathtaking. There was Freddy at the top of the class, and then there was everybody else. Like an academic Michael Jordan, he topped us in physics and religious knowledge, chemistry, scripture, math, literature, English, and Latin. He had no weaknesses. I remember looking in Freddy's notebook once and being awed by the beautifully scripted and copious notes he had taken; I did not think that Freddy even needed to take notes.

Father Feeney, our physics and chemistry teacher, embraced Freddy. One day in chemistry class, Father was discussing the element carbon and surprised us with the fact that charcoal and diamonds were exact chemical equivalents, carbon. This was really hard for us to believe (still is), but Father had said it, and therefore it must be so. Knowing of Father's deep admiration of Freddy, it did not take long for the lads to start referring to him as Father Feeney's Black Diamond.

Yes, the Black Diamond was our hero in the academic arena, and just as the kids of today want "to be like Mike," we wanted to be like Freddy. God bless you, Freddy.

Freddy became a physics professor in both Guyana and the University of the West Indies in Trinidad, no doubt finding and polishing the next generation of Black Diamonds. He died in Trinidad in 2012.

"Series," "Good Morning," and other boyhood diversions

The southern United States is renowned for the courteous behavior of its citizens… "Thank you, ma'am," "Morning, ma'am," etc. How come? The slow Southern drawl is another uniquely regional attribute. Could it be that both characteristics are consequences of prolonged slave-and-slave-owner contact? Like your children, wouldn't you want your slaves to show you the proper deference and respect? "Thanks, massa," "Morning, massa," etc.? And to make sure that like children your language-limited slaves *get it*, wouldn't you speak to them slowly and deliberately? And could it be that over time these practices so permeated the culture that slow speech and mannerly behavior became a Southern norm? I think so.

In Guyana, we *got it*. As the descendants of slaves, we were mannerly to a fault. Adults felt a responsibility to discipline unmannerly children appropriately, whether related to them or not. Not only did such discipline enjoy blanket approval from parents, but also parents usually applied further discipline upon discovery.

The kids got it too. As boys at school, we even created games around behavioral ethics. One such game was "series." You entered a "series" pact with another boy by hooking little fingers and pulling them apart; you also broke a pact the same way. In a series pact, if you used a bad word (curse) and were overheard by pact members, they were at liberty to pummel you unless you said "series" and then whistled. It sounds easy to avoid a sustained pummeling, but trying to whistle while crying out in pain from punches to the shoulder is difficult.

Another such pact, similarly entered, was "good morning." Failure to say "good morning" to a fellow pact member could earn you a punch to the shoulder, which thereby elicited the requisite courtesy. Sometimes you just forgot to say "good morning," but typically, you were blind-sided by lurking pact members. This was not a game for the faint of heart.

Then there was "lab ass," a schoolyard game that could claim no lofty derivation. Simply, a ball was thrown into the middle of the schoolyard during break for the boys to kick. However, while in the process of kicking or otherwise in contact with the ball, you were fair game for a swift kick ("lab") in the rump. Yes, it was mindless, but it was an extremely popular game. Ah, boys will be boys wherever they are.

Christopher

One of my earliest recollections is from around 1940 when we lived off Vlissingen Road in Georgetown, the capital of British Guiana. Many of the streets and places were named during an earlier period when the Dutch occupied British Guiana, as they did in neighboring Dutch Guiana. Anyway, Daddy came bounding up the front steps of our house, built on stilts in recognition that Georgetown is below sea level, in time to hear one of his favorite radio programs. It might have been the Arthur Sylvester program. As he came into the house, Mommy was both inconsolable and in a cold rage. The Nanny, who was responsible for the care of one-year-old Tony, had taken her eyes off him, and he had crawled up into a window flower box and fell out onto the ground, a full story below. Daddy, who had some complex relationships with many of our nannies and maids, was forced to fire her (fig. 54.)

Baby Tony, shortly after his attempt to fly (fig. 54)

Recently, my godmother, Aunt Rene Willock, gave us her own version of the day I was born in September 1937. Mummy, nine months pregnant, was catering some affair or other and had enlisted some of her friends to help, including Aunt Rene, her best friend. Sometime during the day she told Aunt Rene that I was about to make my entrance. The midwife, who didn't live far away, was summoned and promptly dismissed everyone from the bedroom, including Daddy and Aunt Rene. By now, Daddy and Uncle George Willock, Editor of the local newspaper, the *Demerara Daily Chronicle*, were pacing back and forth in the living room. Soon they heard a baby's cry, and the midwife came out and ceremoniously informed Daddy that he had his first son. After muttering, "A son, a son," Daddy fell to the floor in a cold faint and had to be revived. Mummy, who had had a hard birth with my sister Claire, took it all in stride, and was fine.

*****

These were the years of the Second World War. Hitler was marching through Europe unimpeded, and only the British and Winston Churchill stood in his way. As loyal subjects of the British Empire, we Guianese followed Britain's war effort with trepidation and pride. Every schoolboy wanted to be like Winston Churchill, and we roundly scoffed at Neville Chamberlain as a coward. It was 1940 and America hadn't yet entered the war. Unconfirmed reports circulated widely in Georgetown that German U-boats were spotted off the seawall in the Atlantic Ocean.

It was during this period that Daddy, a career colonial government servant to the core, was transferred to the remote Essequibo area as Assistant District Commissioner. Essequibo was the county and district name for an area west of Georgetown which, at the time, could only be accessed by a half day's ferry ride from Georgetown. Daddy's assignment was to implement a nutrition program for children who lived in the interior—that is, the equatorial jungle. Essequibo was an area at the mouth of the Essequibo River that entered the Atlantic Ocean near the government compound where we lived. Our large house was set back about one hundred yards from the main road. The yard was one to two acres and contained every local fruit tree. There were mangoes, sapodillas, five fingers, star apples, limes, papayas, bananas, citrus fruits, guineps, souri, and many others whose names I've long forgotten.

The house came equipped with staff. There was Massa, the gardener, who seemed to stay drunk most of the time. Once, while milking the cow in the pasture, he must have been pretty rough and the cow kicked him in the air, bucket and all. To us kids, it was the most hilarious thing you could imagine. For Massa, his real and imagined injuries kept him in his room for days, and he would complain about his backaches constantly. He took particular delight when we would walk on his back as a kind of physical therapy. Massa's bedroom was right under Tony's and mine, and we had carved a hole at a strategic, hidden spot in the floor to observe Massa's comings and goings. It seemed that, whenever no one was around, Massa miraculously recovered. His limp was gone, he walked erect, and the constant moaning ceased. Like typical boys, we tattled on Massa to our parents, and Massa was immediately back on the job.

Life in Essequibo was generally pleasant. Most afternoons, Daddy made the trip to the regional hospital where Dr. Wailing, a White English doctor, resided, and that had a tennis court where Daddy would play. For as long as I can remember, Daddy was an avid tennis player. His other sport was Bridge, and his lifelong passion was drama (fig. 55). Mummy, who had earlier been a teacher of domestic science, and Director at Government House in Georgetown, served on the Board of Directors of Endeneming House, a correctional house for boys (fig. 56). Also on the board with her were Peggy Wailing, her mother, and Auntie Fields, Dickie Fields's mom. Dickie Fields later headed one of the largest law firms in Guyana and became Queen's counsel. About 1946, when I was nine years old and we had moved back to Georgetown, we lived next door to the Fields family on Laluni Street.

A group of British Guiana's influential leaders ca. 1940s: Bertie Martin (third from left), George Willock (kneeling), Cecil Holmes (sitting), Dr. Claude Denbow (third from right), Ambassador Sir. John Carter, my godfather (extreme right) (fig. 55)

Board of Directors of The Endeneming House: Ruby Martin
(left rear) and Mrs. Fields (rear right standing) (fig. 56)

Essequibo holds so many memories for me. Once, the villagers caught a tiger and paraded his carcass along the road outside our front gate. Another time, we had to walk a few miles to school because something was wrong with either the car or our chauffeur, Mr. Shaw. On the way, we came upon a huge boa constrictor stretched across the road, right in our path. What to do? Claire had the perfect solution. We all hold hands, take a running start and jump over it. On the count of three, that's what we did. It worked and we all lived to tell the tale.

Another time, Mr. Shaw forgot to tighten the tire nuts after a flat tire. It was a Sunday afternoon, and Daddy was driving us all somewhere when all of a sudden we see a tire flying off into a rice field. Boy, was Daddy fit to be tied with Shaw. I can't remember if he fired him, but I don't remember any more Shaw stories. Once there was a fire at the docks near our house that destroyed one of the ferryboats. After all these years, I still hear a man's voice shouting, "Help, Lewis, help!", a cry of anguish that went on all night, the circumstances and consequences of which I never learned.

There was one incident I vividly remember that occurred around 1945, right after the Germans had surrendered to the Allies. We still lived in the big house in Essequibo, and I was around seven or eight. I was beginning to acquire a penchant for reading and a curiosity about events. I had not yet developed my obsession with the Hardy Boys books. That came later. I remember being in the living room, sitting on a Berbice chair under the gas lantern which Daddy pumped up every night at dusk, when a black book caught my eye. I forget the title, or indeed, if it had a title, but I do remember it was quite unadorned and mysterious. I opened the book, and what I saw and read affected me for the rest of my life. It held page after horrific page of human skeletons, alive and dead, stacked like wood or staring blankly into the abyss of the horror they had endured at the hands of the Nazis. I cried that day and cry now as I write this. It was only much later in life that I learned that my grandfather was a German Jew and that I myself am of Jewish heritage.

On the ground floor of our Laluni Street house in Georgetown was a small garage that Tony and I had set up as a chemistry laboratory (fig. 57). Daddy had brought us a chemistry set from his one-year sabbatical in England. My best friend, Colin McDavid, a classmate and neighbor, had set up a physics lab under his house. We alternated experiments between his physics lab and my chemistry lab and thus were easily able to keep up with Father Feeney's lessons in chemistry and physics. Ah, but Tony and I were not mindful of Alexander Pope's advice: "A little learning is a dangerous thing. Drink deep or taste not the Pierian spring. There shallow draughts intoxicate the brain, and drinking largely sobers us again." So Tony and I put some sulfuric acid into a beaker and added zinc (which we had bought with our allowance from Mr. Armstrong, the friendly druggist and source of all our chemicals). We could see the bubbling from the chemical reaction and knew that one of the products from the reaction should be $H2$, hydrogen gas. But how could we be sure? Well, one way was to put a lighted match at the mouth of the beaker. So we did. Mommy came flying down the stairs to see if her two sons were still alive after the explosion "heard 'round the block." Miraculously we were.

121 Laluni Street, location of Chris and Tony's
infamous chemistry lab (fig. 57)

Nearly sixty years later, in 2007, I was visiting Guyana and my dear friends Cathy and Nigel Hughes held a luncheon for Claire and me and our spouses (fig. 58). Dickie Fields and a number of old friends from our youth were there. Dickie then recounted the story of the stir I had caused in the neighborhood so many years ago, and we all laughed. Oh, what a glorious childhood we had growing up in British Guiana.

Luncheon at Cathy and Nigel Hughes' home, Georgetown, 2007. Nigel Hughes, Sam Combs (Claire's husband) and Dickie Fields (fig. 58)

When we returned to Georgetown in 1946, we lived in Grandma's house on New Market Street until we moved to Public Road in Kitty near the home of Cheddi and Janet Jagan. Cheddi Jagan, a US trained dentist, and Linden Forbes Burnham, an Afro-Guianese lawyer, formed the People's Progressive Party and argued successfully before the British House of Commons for Guianese independence. Once, Claire and I were walking to school past the Jagan house, and Dr. Jagan, who was a friend of Daddy's, stopped to pick us up and offered to take us to school. Although he later became President of Guyana, he was rumored to be a rabid Communist, and thus, to us, the feared "Bogeyman." Dr. Jagan could not have been nicer and more caring, a quality Claire and I immediately recognized, and we enjoyed a memorable car ride to school. Not too many years ago, Jagan gave a speech in Newark, New Jersey, during his last election campaign. His knowledge of the history of Guyana, his passionate love of the country, and his plans for it were breathtaking. Unfortunately, success in moving the country into a progressive modern democratic State eluded him as it has his successors.

During the 1950s, Claire and I attended Sacred Heart Roman Catholic School, where my Catholic education and religious training began under the strict discipline of some serious nuns. This Catholic regimen continued through St. Stanislaus College High School under the watchful eye of English, Scottish, and Irish Jesuit priests and the principal, Father Scannell.

One recollection I have from my days at Sacred Heart RC School is of a late afternoon on the playground at the girl's part of the school. Two Portuguese classmates, who were brothers, took turns kicking my ass. Trust me, it was richly deserved. I had a tendency to be a smart-ass and have, unfortunately, retained that quality until this day, except that I have become much more diplomatic and have never been in a fight since.

There was also that time at the lunch table during a heated political discussion with my father. I must have been about sixteen at the time. Out came a smart-ass comment to Daddy, and just as quickly came his fist to my eye, which started to swell immediately. "Bull" Burnett, my lifelong best friend who was at the lunch table, remembers and loves to talk about the incident. Mummy grabbed me, swore unprintable epithets at Daddy while giving him "that look," took me into the kitchen, and applied ice to my wounded eye and pride. The poor man circled the house for two or three days before Mummy let him back in, deeply crestfallen and apologetic. Sure, it was my fault, but that didn't stop me from strutting around for a few days while the swelling healed until Daddy put me back in my place. Thank goodness, there was no DYFS in those days. My dad was a good father.

Around 1950 or 1951, with the recommendation and financial support of Mr. John Fernandes, a prominent Georgetown merchant and dear friend of my mother, I was accepted into St. Stanislaus Jesuit College for boys. I entered second form (second year), having passed the standard exam at Sacred Heart. Getting into this school was highly competitive, and sponsorship by an alumnus was very helpful. I was assigned to Butler House and Father Bose, SJ, Butler's staff leader.

My mother and the principal, Father Scannell, SJ, with whom she frequently negotiated late school fees, attended to my moral and intellectual growth. Mommy made sure Tony and I developed character by having us join the Boy Scouts of British Guiana (fig. 59). For his part, Father Scannell relieved my hesitant, reluctant father of one of his paternal obligations by giving me a hilarious, but to him, serious, explanation of the facts of life. I was, after all, an altar boy, and very innocent and, until that time, had never thought about the subject. Bless his heart, when he described to me that babies are conceived by a water pipe sprinkling a bed of roses to get the plant to flower, I was convinced he had lost his mind.

Chris and Tony in their Boy Scouts of British Guiana uniforms (fig. 59)

St. Stanislaus College. Saints! Seven years, five as a student, one as a prefect, and one as a math teacher (fig. 60). Those glorious years would shape all the best parts of my personality, my intellect, and my spirituality for the rest of my life. I remember halcyon days of house cricket, soccer, and Sports Days, all patterned after English public schools like Eton; of intense studies of physics and chemistry, Latin, calculus (integral and differential); and of Shakespeare and Wordsworth, Shelley, and Milton, always under caring and occasional ruthlessness of the English and Irish Jesuits priests. I remember ferrulas (leather straps like shoe soles, used to inflict corporal punishment on hands and derrieres) and feast days, the constant competition in every aspect of school life between the three houses: Butler House, Galton House, and Etheridge House; the discipline of the prefects, "bumping" and "series," and at the end of it all, the Oxford and Cambridge exams that determined whether you would be going on to university. And best of all, *no* girls to impede our progress to manhood. They had their own schools, and we dated those from the appropriate school. Saints boys dated Ursuline Catholic "Vestal Virgins." Queens College (QC) boys dated Bishop's High School girls, who were more secular. I dated and partied with all four schools, "crashing" quite a few private parties with my posse, Bull ("the Dancer") and Marc Matthews ("the Poet").

Chris in front of St. Stanislaus College, Georgetown (fig. 60)

As I recall, the head prefect at the time was a sixth former who was a Butler man. Prefects, who were primarily sixth formers, ruled the school's discipline outside the classroom. They roamed the halls and the ball fields during breaks, and could issue detention slips. They couldn't order ferrulas, nor could they administer them; only priests could do that. Except for Father Bose, who couldn't bring himself to administer "six of the best" ferrulas to a boy's bottom. The principal, Fr. Scannell, SJ, had excused Fr. Bose, a man of saint-like demeanor, from administering this discipline because of his constant tearful reactions. It was not that Father Bose was weak, by any means. I remember that once, one of my classmates, Tommy Thompson, had an epileptic seizure and fell to the classroom floor. Father Bose put his finger in Tommy's mouth and successfully prevented him from biting off his own tongue.

Father Lynch, on the other hand, loved to order ferrulas and loved to administer them. Like most of the staff, he had a nickname, "Jigs," after the cartoon character in "Maggie and Jiggs." A thin sole was his preference, and "nine of the best" was his number. His fingers were stained from cigarettes, and his breath often smelled of alcohol—wine, I guess. He taught math and Latin and was the staff leader of Etheridge House, our archenemy.

The most feared and most respected priest was Father Marques, "Moujer." He taught upper form math and was wont to keep the whole class after school on the slightest whim. His voice was a deep growl and ponderous, like his walk, and he breathed fear into the smartest, bravest fourth former.

"Martin, come up to the board and prove Pythagoras' theorem... No! No! That's wrong. You all are going to stay in after school. Everyone in this class until you all get it right."

At which point the bell would ring for the next class, and the class would vent their anger at me until the next teacher appeared. Moujer was tough, but let me tell you, all his students became proficient in math, both in high school and later at university. He also taught me, unwittingly, that there was no substitute for excellence, and no excuse not to strive for it. If a system expects mediocrity, it's going to get just that. If it expects excellence, it's going to come darn close to it.

I loved second form, even though we had to wear short pants until we reached "manhood" in fifth form. I loved my khaki shirt and pants, and my blue-and-white striped Butler House tie and cap. Etheridge's green and yellow was too boastful, I thought. I forget Galton House colors. They always seemed to put all the best athletes in Etheridge House, so we didn't envy Galton House as much. Mr. Claude Vieira was our English teacher, and we used a green English vocabulary book from which we had to memorize the meaning of every word and use them daily in sentences and in weekly essays. It was then that I was introduced to the Hardy Boys books, the Harry Potter of our era. Hardy Boy books were devoured, exchanged, and prized. It was our youthful currency. A rare one could cost you a whole week's allowance of one schilling or two not-so-rare books in exchange. Almost without exception, we became proficient in English language and ready for Chaucer, Shelly, Wordsworth, Keats, and Shakespeare in fourth form.

Sports Day! Cricket and soccer matches between houses were important, but Sports Day was the Olympics, the Roman Coliseum and test match cricket between the West Indies and England for the Ashes all rolled into one. It was held once a year at the prestigious Georgetown Cricket Club (GCC). Boys from each house competed against each other by age group. Girls from St. Rose's Ursuline College were given the day off and had to attend. Even some Bishops' girls would attend to watch the gladiators and compete for dates with the winners. Multiple winners would be surrounded by girls congratulating them and coyly inviting them to ask for a date. (Girls couldn't be so bold as to ask for a date in those days.) In second form, all I won was the rope-pulling contest thanks to a huge boy in Butler House (fig. 61). That didn't impress any of the girls compared to winners of the one-hundred-yard dash, the two hundred, the 440, 880, and the mile. High jump was way up there with the one hundred, and I did win that in my senior year when girls had become part of my universe (fig. 62). My father, who until then had shown scant interest in my pursuits, was there prominently on the sidelines making hand signals before each jump. He was a Queens College graduate and, as far as I know, did not distinguish himself in sports other than tennis. His passion was in the performing arts, Greek, and Latin literature.

Butler House winners of the Sports Day rope pulling contest, 1949 (fig. 61)

Chris winning the high jump, 1954 (fig. 62)

If I was lucky, my father would lend me his new car, PD157, to take girls on dates, which involved little more than an exciting evening at a movie or at the ice cream parlor, Brown Betty (fig. 63).

Chris and Bertie's car, ca. 1953 (fig. 63)

Fridays were distinguished by two activities, bumping and benediction. "New Boys," as first and second formers were known, had to be "bumped" before they reached the upper forms and started wearing long pants. The school building was L-shaped, and the space within the L was the playground containing a small cricket field. At the far right corner of the field was a giant mango tree with a deep hole in front, about five feet in diameter, covered almost to the top with sawdust, which was used to soften the impact from the high-jump area. This was the bumping pit. New Boys were caught and grasped by arms and legs, mostly by upperclassmen in their own house, raised in the air three times, "one, two, three," and then dropped into the pit. The priests didn't interfere, and the prefects supervised the bumping to make sure no one was hurt. No one was supposed to reach upper class without having been bumped. It was tradition. No one, that is, except me. Any time I saw bumping going on, I quietly headed for the hills. It didn't hurt that I was also one of Fr. Scannell's favorites and an altar boy, and no one came after me. By the time the head prefect realized I had managed to avoid this mild form of hazing, I was in long pants and not far off from becoming a prefect myself. It was tradition that you didn't bump boys wearing long pants.

Another tradition condoned slapping a boy on the head from behind if he had just gotten a close haircut, but you couldn't tap the head of a boy wearing long pants.

At two o'clock on Friday afternoon, the bell rang, and everyone collected his books and homework for the weekend, got on his bike, and rode the four blocks to Brickdam Cathedral for benediction, no exceptions (fig. 64). If you tried to ride off on a side street to escape benediction, you were halted by a prefect, who, if he was in a bad mood, could write you up for detention the next week. As an altar boy and a prefect, I alternated between benediction and street interceptor duty. On occasion, I was also called upon to read scripture to the priests during their lunch. I looked forward to this duty since the food they had for lunch was always better than my own and included generous portions of ice cream.

Brickdam Cathedral, Georgetown (fig. 64)

"Cricket, Lovely Cricket" was a popular West Indian song when I was in second form around 1950.

> Cricket, lovely cricket, at Lord's where I saw
> it. Cricket, lovely cricket, at Lord's where I saw
> it. The bowling was super fine, Ramhadin and
> Valentine.

The West Indies were playing a four test match series against England at Lords in London, known as "the home of cricket," and owned by the Marylebone Cricket Club. Sir Frank Worrell, Sir Everton Weekes, and Sir Clyde Walcott were the West Indies batting stars. Sonny Ramhadin and Alf Valentine were the spin bowling stars. The West Indies won the series for the first time in history, 3 to 1. Cricket from that time forward became a singular focus for boys like me. The men of that series, the three Ws and Ramhadin and Valentine, were the sports heroes of our time.

In 1954, I was in fifth form and had graduated to long pants. Along the driveway at our home across the street from the Georgetown Cricket Club was a concrete strip where Daddy used to park his car. The driveway was about twenty yards long, almost the length of a cricket "pitch." Tony and I would put a big can or some other obstruction two to three feet wide to act as a wicket. The side of the house would act as an "off leg" side stop for balls hit to the right. Tony would bowl to me until I was out, and then we would reverse the process.

One day Lance Gibbs, a friend and neighbor a couple of years older than I, was walking past the house, stopped, and asked if he could bowl a few balls to Tony. Tony never saw the first ball, which broke sharply right when it hit the ground and hit the wicket. Out. I asked Lance to bowl to me. Same result in two balls. Out. Lance Gibbs, who now lives in Florida, went on to become one of the greatest West Indian Test bowlers in the history of Test cricket. He was one of only two bowlers worldwide in Test cricket history to surpass three hundred test wickets.

The Taitt House (fig. 65)

Basketball, new to Guiana in the 1950s, was also becoming very popular. I was a part of the Panther team, which won the annual championship in 1955. The Panthers practiced at the Taitt house, now a hotel on Murray Street (fig. 65). The Taitt house and grounds were the cultural, social, and athletic center for many middle-class teens in Georgetown. The house was owned by Mrs. Dorothy Taitt, doyenne of the social life of Georgetown, and her husband, Dr. Taitt. On the second floor, above his surgery, was his daughter, Helen, giving ballet lessons, and Hugh Sam, a budding classic musician, composing classical music. In the yard, Dr. Taitt's sons, Clairmonte and Lawrence, had dug two pits in the ground and filled them with sawdust. One was for high-jump practice and the other for a new sporting event introduced into the high school athletic programs, pole-vaulting. Another section of the yard was cleared of Mrs. Taitt's flower gardens to accommodate another new sport in British Guiana, basketball for both boys and girls. The Panthers practiced here, as did the Taitt home team, Ravens and a girls' team, the Flyers. Adding to the cacophony was the steel band, practicing for its next gig. Mrs. Taitt was a major supporter of many of my father's theatrical performances. We rarely saw Dr. Taitt, a man of reticence and anguished patience with all the shenanigans going on around him. He stayed in his surgery and kept his head down (fig. 66, 67).

Panthers Basketball Team (fig. 66)

Flyers Girls' Basketball Team (fig. 67)

Off to the United States

In 1955, I took and passed eight subjects of the Oxford and Cambridge exam, giving me the option to go to University in either the US or Canada. After studying and taking the London University higher-level exams to be eligible to go to a British university, I spent the following year teaching math at Saints to earn money to finance my US education. Father Scannell, through his Jesuit connections, did get me into both Georgetown University and Catholic University in Washington, DC, but I chose Howard University.

Why did I choose the US? It started with the movies. Going to the movies on Saturday in British Guiana was an exciting experience. There was a certain protocol to be observed. If you didn't have a date and wanted to go "on the cheap," you went into "the pits" for a shilling (about a quarter). You had to hide your identity and not let your buddies see you in the cheap seats where the ruffians went. If you had a date and 2 shillings, you could avoid your buddies calling you out in the pits. On special occasions, for about 3 shillings, you went further upstairs into the balcony where you could do some hand-holding and perhaps a little more without being noticed, especially by your boys or the girl you were with the previous week. If you were going by yourself or with your boys, it was usually for a Bela Lugosi horror film. With a date, it would be a cowboy movie with Randolph Scott or a World War II movie like *Back to Bataan* with John Wayne, or perhaps *Halls of Montezuma* with Richard Widmark. In the cowboy and Indian films, we all rooted for the cowboys. No wonder that, when it was time to select the country for my higher education, there was no question. The USA, where I hoped to meet real cowboys. However, I didn't find too many of those in Washington, DC, New York, or New Jersey.

I actually did meet a real cowboy years later when I was overseeing the construction of a chemical plant I had designed for Allied Chemical in Green River, Wyoming. I was confronted by a cowboy on horseback in the usual attire of cowboy hat, dungarees, leather boots, and six-shooters in holsters strapped to his thighs. I was on his land trying to stop Allied's underground waste from seeping into his alfalfa field. I was in seventh heaven. A real, live, breathing cowboy on a horse, no less. Just like Roy Rogers from my boyhood memories. I was very apologetic and explained the solution to the seepage problem to his satisfaction. What a country (fig. 92)!

Green River, Wyoming. Chris' project upstream from the Allied Chemical Corporation Green River Soda Ash plant and the cowboy's farm. (fig. 92)

In July 1957, with $230 US in hand and an acceptance to Howard University's School of Engineering and Architecture, I left British Guiana for the US, with high hopes for a future as a civil engineer. On the trip, I disembarked briefly in Puerto Rico to go through customs and continued on to Idlewild Airport in New York City that night. When I stepped off the plane in Puerto Rico, it was like entering the gates of hell. The heat and humidity was unlike anything I had experienced in British Guiana, where the trade winds have a cooling effect on our very hot ninety-degree weather. Landing at night in New York, with the millions of lights of the city, was a sight I shall never forget. It convinced me that I had made the right choice, not Canada nor Great Britain, my other options.

I spent a few days in Brooklyn at the home of Aunt Lucille Holmes, whose husband, Cecil, was a friend of my father before he moved his family to New York and became a very successful businessman. Their gorgeous daughter, Carol, took me to some of the highlights of New York, like the Empire State Building. My dream of the greatness of America was confirmed, and it never flagged, even after my many personal experiences with racism.

Aunt May Barnwell was Daddy's half sister who lived in Southeast Washington, DC, in a two-bedroom apartment. She was a secretary at the US Department of Commerce, unusual for a person of color. Claire was already living with Aunt May, having completed her first year of college at Howard University. Since I had just enough money to cover my first year of tuition, but not enough to cover room and board, Aunt May agreed to take me in (fig. 68).

Aunt May in front of the U.S. Capitol building (fig. 68)

Two things stick in my memory. The first was sleeping on the couch, my first experience with a convertible. The second, more instructive, learning experience was the food protocol. Having three, and sometimes four mouths to feed on a limited income, was an enormous challenge, but Aunt May made it work. She had a metal cupboard three feet wide by six feet high (not too tall for her since she was almost six feet tall herself) by eighteen inches deep. On these shelves, she kept a plethora of canned goods arranged according to type. Bartlett pears were four or five deep, pork and beans five or six deep, canned spaghetti, sauerkraut, condensed milk, and so on. On the inside of the door was a list of every item in the cupboard with tick marks denoting the number of each can of food. Aunt May told us we could take anything we wanted, but we had to check it off on the list. This gave her an accurate running inventory on what we had left and what had to be replaced. Every Saturday, on her day off, we went to the supermarket and bought in bulk anything that was on sale that we could use—my first introduction to coupons. Thus started my first year of college at Howard.

One incident my aunt May told me about during that first year brought home to me in a striking way the stark difference in race relations between British Guiana and the US. Aunt May was a devout Catholic who went to Mass regularly. However, the first time she tried to attend Mass in Washington, DC, at her neighborhood Catholic church, the priest told her that Negroes were not allowed to worship there. Despite its history of slavery, the country in which I grew up enjoyed a thoroughly ethnically integrated society, and I had never experienced racial discrimination. Aunt May's story was an eye-opener and just the first harbinger of the many encounters with discrimination that I would personally confront in my adopted country.

Given the excellent British-styled education I had received at Saints, it was not surprising that math, English, chemistry, social science, and philosophy came so easily to me at Howard. At the end of October 1957, I met my future first wife, Darlene Bernice Williams, and courted her for three years until we got married at a Catholic church in Washington in black tie and tails (fig. 69, 70). Darlene's father was a prominent DC businessman who spared no expense for the wedding of his daughter to this struggling college senior.

Chris and Darlene, 1960 (fig. 69)

Chris and Darlene at their wedding, 1960 (fig. 70)

Having arrived in the US with virtually nothing in my pocket, I was sustaining myself by working as a bellhop at the prestigious Cosmos Club on the 4:00 p.m. to midnight shift. The Cosmos Club, founded in 1878, was a private hotel/residence for the country's male intellectual elite (no women allowed!). Each member had to have authored at least one book. Senator John Kennedy was a member, as were Dr. Linus Pauling, Andrew Teller, and Wernher von Braun. The job not only gave me income and some memorable late-night meals of lobster and steak when the kitchen closed, but introduced me to some of the best minds in America. It was here that Linus Pauling and Andrew Teller stayed when they were in town for congressional hearings, and it was here that they engaged in heated debates about the future of the atomic bomb, containment of the Soviet Union, and the Cold War. Wernher von Braun would generally avoid the discussion with his usual haughty detachment. Often, when arrivals had slowed down, dinner was over, and I was working on my studies, Dr. Pauling or some other Nobel Prize winner would help me with difficult math problems. I remember Dr. Sears, a historian, suggesting that President Roosevelt knew of the impending Japanese attack on Pearl Harbor well before it occurred but held back this knowledge, knowing that an actual attack on the United States would overcome political opposition to US entry into World War II. I remember Dr. Hauck, another member of the club, and his wife attending my wedding to Darlene (fig. 71).

Chris and Darlene's wedding, 1960 (fig. 71)

After three years at the Cosmos Club, leaving there after my graduation was somewhat bittersweet, and recently, I found a poem I wrote commemorating my three years there (Appendix 3).

Near the end of my first year at Howard, Daddy came to the US on a paid sabbatical to study theater and do some overseas broadcast programming with the *Voice of America*. In those years in British Guiana, civil servants like my father were given six-month paid sabbaticals every four years with government-paid passage and accommodations to any country in the Commonwealth. My plan was to go to New York City for the summer and earn enough money for my $288 in school fees for the following year.

Daddy was very disappointed that I would not be spending the summer with him and his sister at Aunt May's apartment in Washington. Fig. 72 shows us together in front of my aunt's apartment building during his visit. Little did I know that it was the last time I would ever see my father, and I have long regretted that I did not spend the summer with him, as he had wanted me to. He passed away the following year shortly after he returned to British Guiana, and because of the lack of easy communication between the two countries, I did not even learn of his death until a month after his funeral.

Bertie and Christopher in Washington, D.C., 1958 (fig. 72)

That summer at the end of my freshman year was memorable for another reason. I knew that to earn my tuition, I would have to live a very Spartan life. Although I found a job at Rudd Plastic Factory on Coney Island sorting recycled plastic by color, I feared the rent in New York would eat all my earnings. I and two Guianese engineering friends, Jimmy Parks and Neville Softleigh, came up with a solution. We rented a small room off the kitchen in another friend's apartment. The room was just big enough for one single bed and had just enough space on the side to exit the room. The rent, divided by three, was manageable. However, we had to sleep in three shifts and arrange our jobs accordingly. My shift was midnight to eight. That meant eating breakfast as dinner and then returning home to occupy the single bed from 10:00 a.m. to 6:00 p.m. Then I had to vacate it so Jimmy could use it from 6:00 p.m. to 2:00 a.m. Neville got his turn from 2:00 a.m. to 10:00 a.m. Then the bed was mine again. The sheets were changed once a week—plenty for hardworking college students.

My key to food survival was Horn & Hardart, with its huge wall of glass-fronted compartments containing delicious ready-made meals with slots for nickels underneath. Feed in the nickels and the door magically opened, allowing access to the meal. It was America's ingenious innovation for serving "the city that never sleeps." Delicious! What a country!

In 1961, as VP of the Caribbean Association and president of my student chapter of the American Society of Civil Engineers, I was invited with other student leaders to the White House to meet the newly elected president John F. Kennedy and his wife, Jacqueline. A rabid supporter of Kennedy, I had closely followed his career and his debates with Vice President Richard Nixon. Meeting him at the White House was a significant event in my life (fig. 73).

Chris' Invitation to Kennedy Rose Garden Reception, 1961 (fig. 73)

At the end of my sophomore year, my brother Tony joined me at Howard and was my roommate for a while. Tony started out in architecture, as Daddy had decreed, but I convinced him to switch to mechanical engineering for which he was better suited.

After graduation, he became a professional engineer and was the project manager for Terraset in Reston, Virginia, the first solar school to be built in the US that was partially heated and cooled by solar energy. This was in 1977, during the "energy crisis" that marked the Carter administration, and the solar aspects of the school were financed with a $750,000 check from a Saudi Arabian prince and King Saud's philanthropic foundation. In return for the grant from Saudi Arabia, Tony spent a summer lecturing at the University of Petroleum and Minerals in Dhahran.

Tony's distinguished engineering career with the Fairfax County School System included several energy conservation techniques including "heat reclaim" and "computer-controlled energy selection pricing." He really was a pioneer in assisting the nation's efforts to conserve energy.

*****

Other than the usual ups and downs, my college career went fairly well. One event I still painfully recall was when I fainted on the stairs leading to my physics class with the feared Dr. Branson. His was the class that whittled down the number of engineering students to a fraction of the freshman class. Since I was working the four-to-midnight shift, I didn't have time to eat breakfast and make his eight o'clock class. When I came to, guys were stepping over me to get to class. I got up and went to class too.

Another amusing event occurred two weeks before my marriage to Darlene. I had never dated anyone after I met her in my freshman year. It was at the end of my junior year, and my friends threw a party for us. I figured that this was my last opportunity to test the waters, and I danced with another girl for most of the party. Next morning, I got a frantic call from Darlene's mother asking what was wrong. Her daughter was calling off the wedding, on which her parents had already spent a considerable amount. Every day for the next ten days, Darlene received a dozen roses from me (despite my limited income), along with voluminous letters, poetry readings, apologies, and just plain begging. She finally forgave me, and the wedding was back on.

After I graduated from Howard, it took me about a month to realize that getting a good job in the civil engineering field would not be easy because of my noncitizen status. The only interview I landed by attending multiple recruiting fairs at Howard was with a Cleveland utility company that was not interested in a foreign student graduate. So I travelled to New York City and started going to employment agencies in and around the Times Square area. I started at 9:00 a.m. and went from agency to agency until 5:00

p.m., closing time, without success. I was about to quit and get a bus back to DC, but there was one door left—an agency on a second floor walkup. I tried to open the door, but it had just been locked.

In desperation, I started banging on it until I heard a voice inside shouting, "What is it?"

I shouted back, "I'm a recent civil engineering graduate from Howard University, and I'm looking for a job."

"Hold on, son, I'll let you in," a voice responded.

The door opened, and I got a job as a trainee with Allied Chemical Corporation, with which I subsequently enjoyed a twenty-year career.

Part of the reason that I, an Afro-Guianese noncitizen, got the job was due to a new initiative by recently elected president Kennedy, "Plans for Progress," which encouraged companies to hire minority engineers. The starting salary was $525 a month, and I said to Darlene, my new wife, "What are we going to do with all that money?" What a country!

Deryck was born a little over a year after we were married, and Mike came thirteen months after that (fig. 74). It was then that Darlene's health deteriorated, and our whole world turned upside down when an eye doctor at St. Michael's Hospital in Newark diagnosed her with the then-incurable disease, multiple sclerosis. He told us she would be dead within a year.

Chris' family ca. 1967. Rear l-r: Chris, Tony, Tony's first
wife, June, Claire's first husband, Fred; front l-r: Michael,
Darlene, Mummy, Claire, Deryck (fig. 74)

Life after that was not the same. Darlene and I divorced in 1976
when Deryck was fifteen and Mike was fourteen. Shortly after that,
Darlene was admitted to Morris View Nursing Home, where she
spent her remaining years. She passed away more than thirty years
after her initial diagnosis. She was a remarkable woman in every
way—kind, spiritual, loving, and with an indomitable will to live
despite the lousy hand she had been dealt. I loved her very much.

When Darlene and I first moved to Morristown, we had a difficult time finding a place to live because of racial discrimination
in housing. This led me into protest politics, not unusual for Black
professionals in the 1960s. Together with Dr. James Lassiter, my
dentist, and Norman Lattimore, the preeminent Black politician in
Morristown and my mentor and best friend, we redistricted the town
to create a majority Black ward, and Jimmy and I became the first
Black Americans in history to sit on the Town Board of Aldermen
(figs. 75, 76, 77). Since that time, there have always been at least two
African Americans on the seven-member Town Council.

Newark Evening News

WEDNESDAY, MARCH 1, 1967   21

Drawn by NAACP

Morristown Given Redistricting Plan

By THEODORE FEUREY
Staff Correspondent.

MORRISTOWN—A local redistricting plan, calling for five wards in place of the present four, was unveiled last night.

The plan, one of four prepared by the Morris County Chapter of the National Association for the Advancement of Colored People, has been proposed to end population imbalance existing under the present system.

Mayor Victor Woodhull, a Republican, and Democratic Alderman Theodore Goodman expressed guarded approval of the plan, but neither would give it outright support.

Committee Asked

Both, however, praised the NAACP chapter "for providing the impetus for a much-needed reapportionment study."

The presentation came in the wake of a motion unanimously adopted by the Board of Aldermen Monday night calling for immediate formation of a reapportionment study committee.

Woodhull said he has already asked Town Attorney Myron Bromberg to prepare a memorandum on the legal aspects of a reapportionment commission. He said he would probably request Bromberg to begin the drawing of an ordinance at a conference meeting Tuesday.

60-Day Report

Under state statute, a reapportionment committee, created by ordinance and consisting of two Republicans and two Democrats appointed by the mayor, would have 60 days to present a reapportionment plan to the town clerk.

The plan, approved by the commission, would become law.

Norman O. Lattimore, chairman of the NAACP committee that produced the four proposals, said all the proposals and accompanying statistics would be presented to the reapportionment commission.

"The NAACP is asking nothing," he said. "We have done the work, the commission may use it, adapt it, or disregard it. These plans are little more than suggestions."

Statistical Base

Christopher L. Martin, who supervised most of the actual tabulation in the redistricting studies, said population distribution and voting patterns of the town have been under study for more than two years.

Under the present ward system, the 1st and 2d wards have nearly three times the population of the 3d and 4th wards. Under the five-ward proposal, each of the wards would contain about 1,800 voters.

The proposed 5th Ward would be composed of the 5th and 6th districts of the 1st ward and the 1st and 2d districts of the 2d Ward.

The other two wards would remain essentially the same. Lines would be redrawn throughout the town, however, to create 21 instead of the present 18 voting districts.

Newark Evening News article regarding Morristown Redistricting (fig. 75)

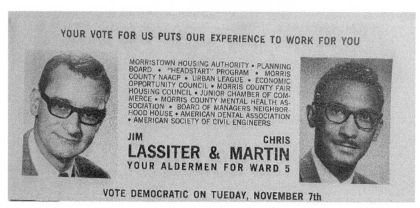

Election flyer for James Lassiter, DDS, and Chris Martin, 1967,
running for Morristown Board of Aldermen (fig. 76)

Chris and Morristown Mayor Marco Stirone (fig. 77)

Working together with White members of the Morristown Fair Housing Council, we tested local apartments and were able to prove that landlords regularly refused to rent to Black couples while willingly renting to similarly situated Whites. Armed with this proof, we presented our case to the legislature and the courts and were able to get legislation passed in New Jersey that made it unlawful to discriminate in housing. From then on, my involvement in local and state politics escalated. (fig. 78).

Anita and Chris join U.S. Senator Bill Bradley at fund-raising dinner for N.J. Governor Robert Meyner's re-election, ca. 1974 (fig. 78)

The 1960s were heady and contentious years in Morristown and throughout the U.S. but, after much pain and heartache, we changed the country for the better (fig. 79).

Alderman Christopher Martin, Chairman of Morristown Redevelopment Committee, with U.S. Senator Harrison Williams and Mayor Marco Stirone, speaking at a groundbreaking ceremony for "1776 on the Green," the first building erected in Morristown's Redevelopment Project (fig. 79)

One amusing event for me was when, at the request of some Drew University students, I helped to integrate a local White barbershop which had refused haircuts to African Americans and students from India. When Bob Myers, a White member of the Fair Housing Council, and I entered the shop, we acted as though we didn't know each other. The barber proceeded to sharpen his strop razor, while I sat there with the hair on my neck standing straight up. I prayed a lot and came out alive, but he butchered my hair. I had to go directly to my own barber to correct the damage, and Bob and I had a great laugh. We became good friends after that.

As a result of my protest activity on the weekends and my job as a buttoned-down civil engineer during the workweek, an artistic friend made a hilarious poster showing a revolutionary with a wild Afro hairdo and a fierce, angry look fighting off a machine gun. The caption below read, "For revolution, call Chris Martin—weekends only" (fig. 80).

"Super Martin For Revolution" cartoon (fig. 80)

On December 24, 1976, Anita Kastner Hotchkiss, a trial law-yer, and I were married at the Methodist Church on the Green in Morristown (fig. 81). In an extraordinary coincidence, we had both been married the first time on the same year, date, and time of day in cities two hundred miles apart. Our over forty-four years together have been a wonderful journey of discovery. The difference in our races has never been an issue for us or for my two sons or Anita's two daughters, who were often together growing up.

Anita and Chris' wedding, 1976 (fig. 81)

CHAPTER 12

Conclusion

Some people say that you should not spend the last part of your life dwelling on the beginning. Now, in my eighties, I look back and analyze my triumphs, my failures, and my sadness. But I also unabashedly look forward to my nineties, when my great-grandchildren will be largely grown and I will exult in their accomplishments and help guide them through their pain. As Shakespeare so eloquently mused: "The end crowns all. And that old common arbitrator, Time, will one day end it" (fig. 82–91).

Robert Steidlitz (Chris' son-in-law), Deryck
(Chris' son), and Tony Martin (fig. 82)

Vickey Martin (Chris' granddaughter) and Dr. Robert
Llanos at their wedding, 2008 (fig. 83)

Chloe Llanos and her father, Dr. Robert Llanos (fig. 84)

Cousin Tara Smith, Verlyn and Michael Martin (Chris' son
and his wife), Deryck, Vickey and Robert Llanos (fig. 85)

Chris, Verlyn, Michael, Anita, Deryck, Chloe,
Vickey, Alex and Robert Llanos (fig. 86)

Alex Martin, Chris' grandson (fig. 87)

Anita and daughters, Kirsten and Kari, at Vickey's wedding (fig. 88)

Claire, Anita, and Ruth Martin (Tony's wife) at Vickey's wedding (fig. 89)

Anita, daughter Kari, and grandchildren Erik and Elizabeth making
chocolate-covered strawberries, Christmas, ca. 2012 (fig. 90)

Chloe and Alex Llanos, Chris' great grandchildren,
in front of their home (fig. 91)

We started this search for my mother's father, who, by all accounts, was "a German Jewish diamond merchant," and I believe we found him. But more importantly, I found myself. I found a man with my father's too-often unseemly arrogance and impatience, but also his love of British poetry, drama, and classical music. He had an abiding distaste for colonialism, and particularly South African Apartheid. "Suid Afrika Delenda Est" (South Africa must be destroyed) was his constant refrain. And as I later learned, as a student in E. Franklin Frazier's class, "The Impact of Western Civilization on Africa," at Howard. It was Frazier's mantra as well. This disdain for authoritarianism accounts for my immersion in politics and public service in Morristown.

From my mother, I learned all that may have been good in me and little that was bad. My many faults were of my own making. Mummy's kind and generous nature reminds me of the Alfred Beit described in Fort's *Alfred Beit: A Study* (57), a man whose generosity to all was prodigious. I like to think I have inherited all these good qualities to counteract my many bad ones.

This search has also led me to the discovery of many of the Beit family heirs and descendants. Most notable of those I have contacted are Sir

145

Alan Munro, President of The Beit Trust, and his brother Neil, who also then put me in touch with a Beit cousin, Dr. Carter Nance. Amazingly, Dr. Nance lives in Chatham, New Jersey, just east of Morristown.

This is, by no means, the end of our quest. Like many stories and discoveries of this kind, there remain sources, people, and information yet undiscovered. For example, there are many, many pages of unpublished documents in the possession of Neil Munro, Alfred's great nephew of Wimbledon, England, which I have not yet been able to review, as well as other records in the possession of Eric Zinow, a grandchild of Alfred's sister, Bertha. But the story needed to be written.

Around Christmas, 2019 my good friend from Saint Stanislaus and Howard, Rae Hazlewood, and I were reminiscing about our years growing up in British Guiana and how fortunate we were to have had such wonderful early years. I told Rae of my reluctance to write a biography that was neither significant to others outside my family nor interesting to a broader audience. Rae is an economist who spent fourteen years in Africa advising and assisting developing countries there. He has written and published an instructive and acclaimed book on his experiences in Africa, as well as a children's book about Africa. Responding to my reluctance, he quoted a group of Jewish victims of Hitler's atrocities as saying: "And who shall write our history?" No one can write our stories but ourselves. And they did. And I have.

I look forward to meeting those additional living relatives of Alfred's who may or may not be mine as well, but I also look backward. As Leo Martin wrote in the first verse of his poem "Looking Back:"

> It is good, on gaining every station
> In life's progressive day
> To pause a little while in contemplation
> And mark the travelled way.
> Look backward o'er the pathway in the distance,
> And view each stumbling stone,
> To gather fresh experience for resistance
> Of griefs we knew alone.

> *Leo*

THE END

ACKNOWLEDGMENTS

This book was inspired by the sacrifices our parents made to motivate their three children to go to college and have successful professional careers. Their sacrifices, and particularly our mother's, led us on a thirteen-year search to find the identity of the father Mummy never knew.

I am indebted to my late sister, Claire, whose conversations with Mummy gave us invaluable clues to start our search; my brother, Tony, whose early exhaustive research moved us closer to a possible identity; my wife, Anita, a trial lawyer and reference librarian; Anita's equally talented daughter, Kirsten; and my granddaughter, Victoria, all of whom did an enormous job of editing an initially flawed manuscript. And to my son, Deryck, whose extensive computer skills enhanced the manuscript's research effort. I must also credit my friend from high school in Guyana and college, Leyland Hazlewood, an economist who spent fourteen years in Africa and who gave me the encouragement and courage to write our story.

BIBLIOGRAPHY

Albrecht, Henning, tr. by Sir Alan Munro. *Alfred Beit, The Hamburg Diamond King.* Hamburg U. Press, 2012.

Allicock, Dmitri with Christopher Jeffrey. "Historical Guyana in Pictures." 2014. www.guyaneseonline.files.wordpress.com/2014/06/historical-guyana-in-pictures-dmitri-allicock.pdf.

Auerbach, Geraldine MBE. "Alfred Beit—South Africa's financial genius." *Jewish Gen Kehila Links.* London, 2017. http://kehilalinks.jewishgen.org/kimberley/Alfred_Beit.html, 2017.

Banham, Martin, Errol Hill, and George Woodyard. *The Cambridge Guide to African and Caribbean Theatre.* Cambridge U. Press.

Colvin, Ian. *The Life of Jameson.* Edward Arnold & Co., 1922.

British Guiana Journals. Colonial Office Record Book. Vol. 105, 1902. National Archives, Kew Gardens, England.

Colonial Office Record Books, 1900, 1902, 1903. National Archives, Kew Gardens, England.

Combs, Claire Martin, and Paula Matthews Hazlewood. *When We Grew Up in the Land of the Mighty Roraima.* Ex Libris Corporation, 2007.

Dabydeen, David. Intro. Egbert Martin. *Selected Poems.* 2010.

"Diamond Industry's Growth." *New York Times,* 3/1/03.

Epstein, Edward Jay. *The Diamond Invention.* 1982. https://edwardjayepstein.com/diamond/prologue.htm. Accessed 5 Nov. 2020.

—. *The Rise and Fall of Diamonds: The Shattering of a Brilliant Illusion.* Simon and Schuster, 1982.

Fort, G. Seymour. *Alfred Beit: A Study.* Ivor Nicholson & Watson, 1932.

Harrison, John Burchmore. *Geology and the Goldfields of British Guiana*. Dulau, London, 1908.

Josiah, Barbara, P. *Migration, Mining and the African Diaspora*. Palgrave, Macmillan, 2011.

Kirke, Henry. *Twenty-Five Years in British Guiana*. Sampsis Low, Marston & Company, 1898.

Kanfer, Stefan. *The Last Empire: DeBeers, Diamonds, and the World*. Farrar, Straus and Giroux, 1993.

Lee, Robert. *Tewin Water, Welwyn, Hertfordshire. A Brief History of the House, the Estate and the Families Who Lived There*. Heritage Group Development Ltd., 2000.

Lockhart, J.G. and Sir Alfred Beit. *The Will and the Way*. Longmans, Green and Co., 1957.

Martin, Egbert. *Selected Poems*. Ed. by David Dabydeen. The Caribbean Press, 2010.

—. *Leo's Poetical Works*. 1883.

—. *Scriptology*. 1885.

—. *Leo's Local Lyrics*. 1886.

Meredith, Martin. *Diamonds, Gold, and War*. Simon & Schuster, UK, 2007.

Mitford, Deborah. Duchess of Devonshire. *Wait for Me*. Farrar, Straus and Giroux, 2010.

Morrison, Allen. "The Tramways of Georgetown, British Guiana." *Electric Transport in Latin America*. www.tranz.com, 2008. Accessed 20 Nov. 2020.

Petry, Grace. "The Professional Woman." *Schenectady Gazette,* 1988.

Swiecki, Rafal. "Diamonds in Venezuela and Guyana; Historical Review of Diamond Geology and Mining." *Alluvial Exploration and Mining*. www.minelinks.com/alluvial/diamondGeology41.html. Accessed 1/25/08.

Taylor, J. B. *Lucky Jim. Memoirs of a Randlord*. Ed. by T. S. Emslie. (Orig. pub. as *A Pioneer Looks Back*. Hutchinson & Co., 1939). Stonewall Books, 2003.

The People of Tewin Water. *The History of Tewin Water*. Tewin Orchard in association with the Tewin Society History Association, 2009.

Thomasson, Frank. *The History of Theatre in Guyana, 1800–2000.* Hansib Publications, 2009.

Trevelyan, Raleigh. *Grand Dukes and Diamonds: The Wernhers of Luton Hoo.* Faber and Faber, 2012.

Walker, H. De Rosenbach. *The West Indies and the Empire.* E. P. Dutton and Co., 2018.

APPENDIX 1

Tony's timeline of Alfred Beit's Life (1853–1906)

ALFRED BEIT LIFE EVENTS TIMELINE						
EVENT	YEAR	MONTH	DAY	LOCATION	SOURCE	REMARKS
Birth of Alfred Beit	1853	Feb	15	Hamburg, Germany	Wikipedia	Eldest son, 2nd child of affluent Jewish trader.
Birth of Cecil Rhodes	1853	Jul	5	Bishop's Stortford, Hertfordshire, England	Wikipedia	5th son of Rev. Francis William Rhodes, a Church of England vicar
Beit is sent to Cape Colony by Lippert & Co.	1875				Albrecht 136	Sent as Lippert representative to buy diamonds following their discovery in Kimberley.
Beit meets Cecil Rhodes	1879				Albrecht 136	They become close friends and business partners
Beit extends business interests	1886			Kimberley, South Africa		Founds Robertson Syndicate and Wernher, Beit & Co.
Beit's daughter "Queenie" is born	1888			London	Albrecht 24	Illegitimate daughter, Olga (Queenie) by Elizabeth Bennett of Kimberley.
DeBeers Consolidated Mines Ltd. is founded	1888			South Africa	Albrecht 136	With Cecil Rhodes and Barney Barnato, amalgamates 97% of Kimberley diamond interests

Beit becomes life-governor of DeBeers	1888			South Africa	Wikipedia. Albrecht 52	Also becomes partner in Jules Porges & Co. and made director of Rand Mines, Rhodesia Railways, & Beira Railway Company
Beit moves to London, maybe already "the world's richest man"	1888			London, England	Albrecht 136	To better manage his financial empire and support Rhodes's S. African ambitions
The British South Africa Co. (BSAC) is founded	1889			South Africa	*Wikipedia*	With Cecil Rhodes; granted Royal Charter
Beit takes out insurance policies applied for in 1888	1890			London, England	*NY Times* 7/19/1906	With the Equitable Life Assurance Society (US). Beit's will included $70,000 for Elizabeth Bennett "my intended wife"
Jules Porges & Co. becomes Werner Beit & Co.					Albrecht 136	
Beit Travels to S. Africa?	1891			Dartmouth, England	Findmypast. com	From steamer passenger list
Beit returns from S. Africa?	?					
Beit travels to S. Africa?	1895			London, England	Findmypast. com	From steamer passenger list
Jameson raid	1895	Dec	29	Transvaal, South Africa	Wikipedia	
Beit travels by steamer to unknown location	1896			Plymouth, England	Findmypast. com	From steamer passenger list. Not sure if entry was our Alfred Beit
House of Commons Inquiry re: Jameson Raid	1897	May	28	London, England	*NY Times* 5/29/1897	Henry Labouchere led hostile questioning of Beit on Jameson Transvaal raid before a Parliamentary Committee
Mediterranean Cruise	1898				Albrecht *The Hamburg Diamond King*	After the completion of the trial and of his house in London, Beit set off on a three-month cruise to recuperate on a chartered yacht *Iolaire*

Beit's wedding to Mary Moore to be announced	1898	Feb	5	London, England	*NY Times* 2/5/1898	Did not happen. She was an actress, daughter of parliamentary agent Charles Moore, and widow of James Alberry
Beit obtains British Citizenship	1898	Mar	30		London Gazette, 5/3/1898	
London Stock Market activity	1898	May	14	London, England	14 May 1898, Exeter and Plymouth Gazette	
Where was Alfred Beit?	1898	Jul-Sep				The period when Ruby Pollard was conceived—she was born 5/19/1899. Walter Joseph Sendall was Governor.
West Indies. Hurricane	1898	Sep	10 to 12		*Morning Post* 9/22/98	Wernher, Beit hurricane aid contribution in the West Indies
Beit takes a trip to Berlin	1899	Oct	31	Berlin, Germany	*NY Times* 11/1/1899	Pushing for industrial development in Germany and East and Southwest Africa
Second Boer war starts	1899			South Africa	Wikipedia	War ended in 1902. First Boer war was 1880–1881
Beit meets with Rhodes coming from S. Africa	1900	Apr	Circa 6	Funchal, Madeira	*NY Times* 4/7/1900	Beit and Rutherford Harris met with Rhodes prior to his going to London to advise him to be reticent on S. African affairs there
S. Africa Assoc. annual dinner	1900	May	9	London, England	News clip	Speech by Col. Denison with Lord Windsor presiding. Beit, Rutherford Harris and Lionel Phillips were in attendance
Beit meets Rhodes coming from S. Africa	1901	Jul	20	Southampton, England	*NY Times* 7/20/1901	Rhodes and Jameson met by Beit and others

Death of Cecil Rhodes	1902	Mar	26	Muizenberg, S. Africa	Wikipedia	Born 7/5/1853 in England. Buried in Matopos Hills, Zimbabwe (Rhodesia)
Beit travels to S. Africa	1902			Southampton, England	Findmypast. com	From steamer passenger list
Beit leaves for England	1903	Jan	22	Johannesburg, South Africa	*NY Times* 1/23/1903	Recently recovered from serious illness
Beit wrote his last will	1905	Apr	4	London, England	*NY Times* 7/21/1906	Establishes The Beit Trust
Death of Alfred Beit	1906	Jul	16	Tewin Water, near Tewin, Hertfordshire, England	Wikipedia	After suffering a rapid deterioration in his health
Family inheritance	1906	Jul	18	London, England	*NY Times* 7/19/1906	Beit's several married sisters in Germany and Austria, and his mother and brother inherited considerable sums
Wernher, Beit & Co. dissolved	1912	Jan	1	London, England	*NY Times* 1/2/1912	Company dissolved 12/31/1911. Diamond branch transferred to L. Breitmeyer & Co.

APPENDIX 2

Letter from Alfred Beit
to Cecil Rhodes

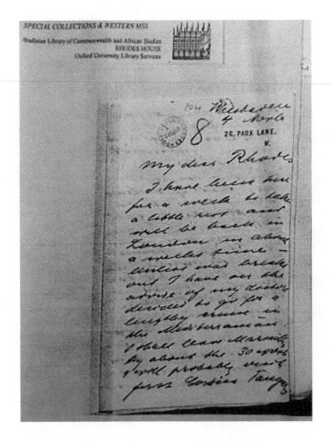

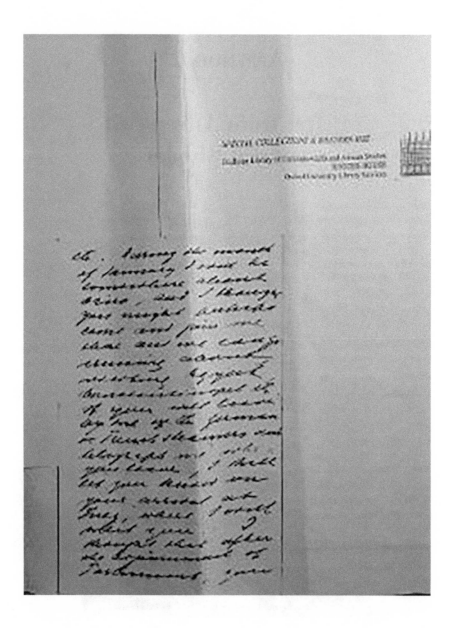

would probably visit
Rhodesia, and I
should say, that you
might be ready to
leave Beira by
about the middle
or end of Decr. —
Please wire me
a word, and if
you don't wish
me to talk about
your plans to
anyone, add the
word private —
I shall probably get
Donald Currie's, actg
about 750 tons and
we will have every
comfort. —
I don't believe in stars
but it is a cast iron

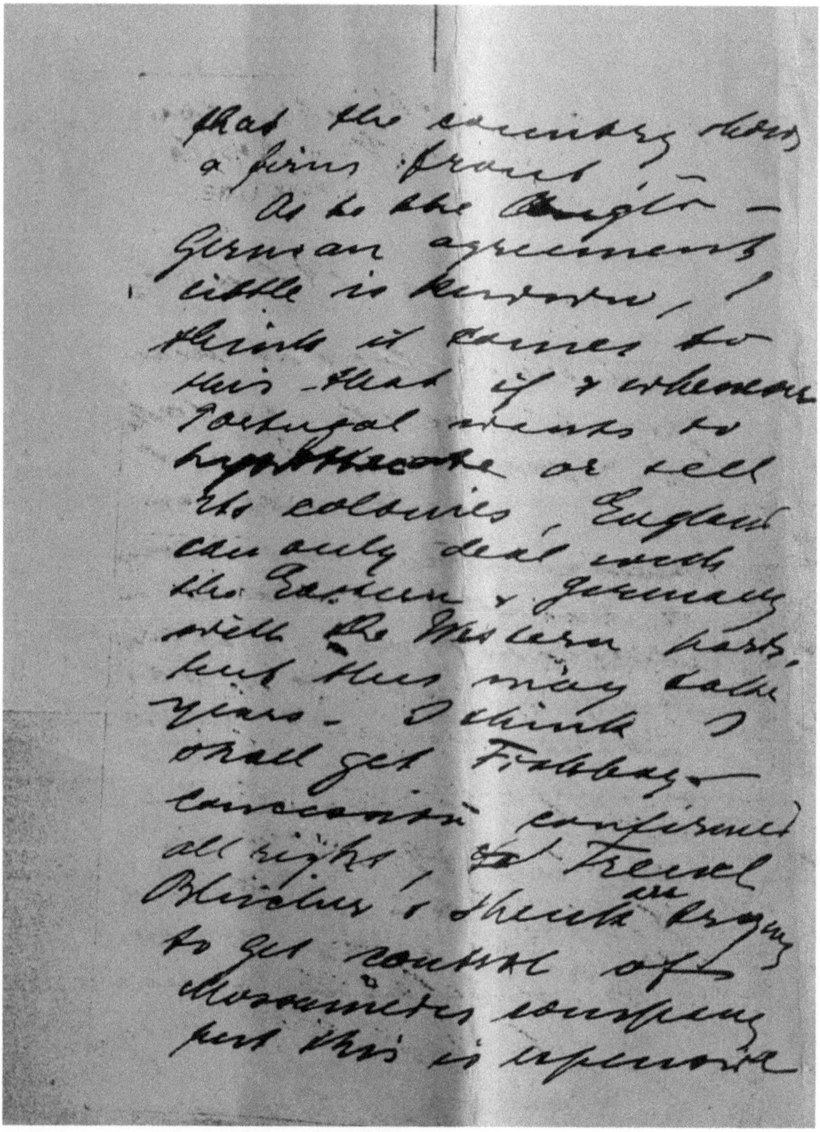

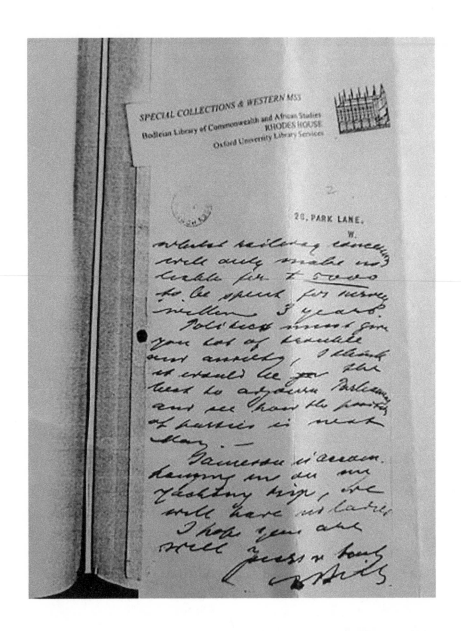

APPENDIX 3

Poem written upon Chris Martin's departure from his job at the Cosmos Club (on Cosmos Club Letterhead), 1961.

To the Members of the Cosmos Club:

TOMORROW IN THE SUNLIGHT

'Tis now twilight and I must take my leave
Humbly, for I have been among intellectual giants,
   It still seems incredible
That these same giants with their PhD's
Have given such great encouragement to me,
What is it about men of learning
That a student like myself received their understanding?
I note they never parade their wit
For they know a little learning is a dangerous thing.
I should guess that when a man becomes a giant
He glimpses sights of truth as yet unknown
Which those less elevated cannot discern.
Enough of this before I ramble,
My main interest was to bid adieu
So let's be on our way now,
The Cosmotographers have their meeting in the Auditorium
And Doctor Webb is anxious to look at television.
What's this about a man who's lost his glove?
My dear man you are in the Cosmos Club
And such things are the common fare.
They'll set it right tomorrow I'll wager.

Is That You, Grandpa?

Did you say it was snowing, Sir?
I really must leave and trudge thru the snow
Like Fra Lippo Lippi rapping on doors
Until I find a refuge for the night.
No, don't worry, I'm sure I'll be all right.
You see, tomorrow promises to be fair
    And I've got things to do
            Tomorrow in the sunlight.

Christopher Martin ('61)
Bellhop turned Civil Engineer

APPENDIX 4

Martin/Beit Family Trees

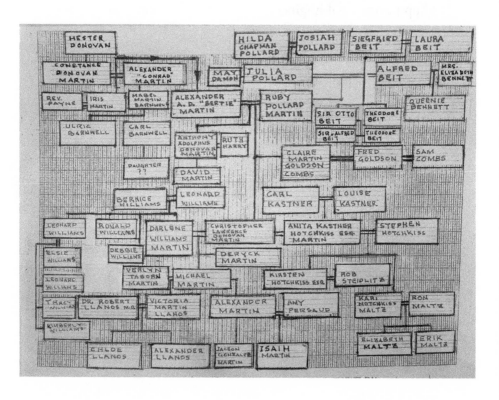

Praise For "Is That You, Grandpa?"

"The scion of a wealthy Hamburg family, financing of diamond and gold mines in South Africa, and a decision of the British Parliament that moves the action through the end of nineteenth-century America and Guyana, South America. The author's meticulous research describes an intriguing and heartwarming journey of discovery into his ancestry." Leyland (Rae) Hazlewood, author of *The Ultimate Guide to Doing Business in Africa*.

"I thoroughly enjoyed the book, especially the recollections of boyhood in British Guiana—a world unfamiliar to me—and I say to Chris Martin 'yasher ko'akh' (Hebrew for 'a great job')."—Erika Leviant

ABOUT THE AUTHOR

Born in British Guiana, South America, Christopher Lawrence Donovan Martin immigrated to the United States in 1957 to attend Howard University. He graduated in 1961 with a degree in civil engineering and became a United States citizen. At Howard he was president of the student chapter of the American Society of Civil Engineers and worked nights as a bellhop at the prestigious Cosmos Club.

In 1961, Chris joined Allied Chemical Corporation and moved to Morristown, New Jersey, where he worked for twenty years designing and building chemical plants.

For fifteen years before his retirement in 1999, he was the Director of Engineering and Maintenance for the Morristown Housing Authority. Always active in civic and community affairs, he was the first Black American on the Board of Aldermen and was instrumental in redeveloping the town's central business district. As President of the Board of Education, he oversaw a $15M expansion of Morristown High School.

Since 2013, Chris and his siblings have been researching the identity of his maternal grandfather.

He currently lives in Morristown with his wife of forty-four years.

To contact the author or comment on this life story, go to www.isthatyougrandpa.com.

CPSIA information can be obtained
at www.ICGtesting.com
Printed in the USA
BVHW031809091121
621205BV00005B/48